THE ART of HOODOO CANDLE MAGIC

CATHERINE YRONWODE

AND

MIKHAIL STRABO

CANDLE MAGIC FOR
THE HOME PRACTITIONER

SPIRITUAL CHURCH
CANDLE SERVICE MANUAL

HOW TO CONDUCT
A CANDLE LIGHT SERVICE

Missionary Independent Spiritual Church
Forestville, California

→ 2013 ←

THE ART OF HOODOO CANDLE MAGIC
IN ROOTWORK, CONJURE, AND SPIRITUAL CHURCH SERVICES
© 2013 Missionary Independent Spiritual Church

Including the following previously published material:

Selected extracts from "Hoodoo in Theory and Practice" by catherine yronwode
"Candle Magic and Types of Candles" **LuckyMojo.com/candlemagic.html**
"Love Magic," "Green Devil," "Break Up," and other spells **LuckyMojo.com/hoodoo.html**
"Candle Magic Divination" **LuckyMojo.com/candlemagicdivination.html**
© 1995-2012 catherine yronwode; reprinted by permission

"The Lucky Mojo Free Spells Archive" **LuckyMojo.com/spells.html**
© 1995-2012 catherine yronwode; reprinted by permission

"Candle Service Manual" by Reverend catherine yronwode
© 2007-2011 Missionary Independent Spiritual Church

"Candle Spells" by catherine yronwode
from the AIRR Web Site **ReadersAndRootworkers.org/wiki/Category:Candle_Spells**
© 2009 catherine yronwode / Association of Independent Readers and Rootworkers / MISC

"Some Thoughts About Candles" by catherine yronwode
from the "The Black Folder" of the MISC Hoodoo Training Workshops
© 2011-2013 catherine yronwode / Missionary Independent Spiritual Church

"How To Conduct a Candle Light Service" by Mikhail Strabo
© 1943 Sydney J. R. Steiner; revised by catherine yronwode

Text:
catherine yronwode, Mikhail Strabo (Sydney J. R. Steiner), Adele Clemens

Artwork:
Charles C. Dawson, charlie wylie, Mikhail Strabo (Sydney J. R. Steiner)

Production:
nagasiva yronwode, charlie wylie, Fred Burke

Illustrations:
Plain and figural candles, 1935-1945   15
A moving candle spell in progress   45
Spiritualist church hall and altar layouts   82

First Edition 2013 / Second Edition 2014 / Third Edition 2015

Published by
Missionary Independent Spiritual Church
6632 Covey Road
Forestville, California 95436
MissionaryIndependent.org

ISBN: 978-0-9836483-6-9

Printed in Canada.

CONTENTS

DEDICATION

This book is dedicated to Charles C. Dawson ("the good artist") and to "Mikhail Strabo," "Henri Gamache," "Lewis De Claremont," "Godfrey Spencer," "Anna Riva," "Charmaine Dey," and all of the other candle shop proprietors, authors, and spiritual workers who hid their identities behind pseudonyms during the era of my youth — because researching their true names has given me so many hours of fun.

ACKNOWLEDGEMENTS

I would like to thank the following people for their help:

My husband nagasiva yronwode for his love and devotion, for daily supplying me with coffee and chocolate, for making pre-war acoustic blues and country music available at all times, for keeping our computers up and online, and for editing, book design, and production on all of my books, including this one.

The Art Department, in the person of the talented charlie wylie.

My animal friends Sophie, Copper Kitty, Kitty Boy Floyd the Outlaw Oklahoma Knew Him Well, The Twa Corbies, Spinner, Sing, Hattie "The Buck-Buck Girl" Hudson, and Reverend Sonny Boy "The Frizzly Rooster" Watson Junior.

My apprentice and friend Johannes Gardback for his noble dedication to the practice of candle magic, which spurred me on to create the original MISC Candle Service Manual in 2007.

Katrina Mead, Lou Florez, and Elvyra Curcuruto-Love, the current deacons and candle servers of Missionary Independent Spiritual Church, who uphold and sustain the work of "The Smallest Church in the World" on a daily basis, with much deftness and devotion.

Maryann Allbright, Ferne Aycock, Sienna Baratti, Susie Bosselmann, Chelsa Burford, Reggie Burford, Alicia Cashaw, Cindy Clark, Avida Cleveland, Leslie Anne Cooper, Celeste Davidson, Oran Davis, Diana Edler, Eileen Edler, Clairissa Elizalde, Pierrette Fitzgerald, Vivian Freeman, April Gibson, David Gravel, Shawna Gray, Tanisia Greer, Edward Grogan, Gwen Gunheim, Brian Hosley, Carin Huber, Amber Hunze, Yelena Kisler, Louise Lieb, Gracie Lock, Elantari Love, Leslie Lowell, Tracy McClendon, Frances McCorkle, Aileen McLeod, Della Mead, Ernie Medeiros, Christopher Murphy, Annette Neal, Artemisia Noble, Leah Ocean, Aidan O'Ryan-Kelly, Lynette Parkerson, Robin Petersen, Ian Philips, Nicole Planchon, Jagat Rainbow, Daniel Reynolds, Roy Ridgley, Don Roach, Rosie Rodriguez, Justin Rose, Julie Sage, Marcella Salisbury, Nicole Sanborn, Karl Schoelles, Loben Simmons, Heidi Simpson, Kate Spellman, Angela Stanfield, David Stolowitz, Juan Trevino, Chelsea Turrone, Lisa Warrick, Kathy Weir, Greg Wharton, Brandon Wilson, Karen Wilson, Nikki Wilson, Yosé Witmus, Kamala Wolf, Andrew Woodruff, Robin York, and others at the Lucky Mojo Curio Company who have unloaded hundreds of tons of candles from freight trucks and set prayer-lights for thousands of grateful clients for the past 20 years.

The Association of Independent Readers and Rootworkers, and especially the AIRR Tech Team members Prof. Charles Porterfield, Lara Rivera, Miss Bri, Deacon Millett, ConjureMan Ali, and Dr. E. for editorial help with the portion of this text first published on the AIRR web site.

My colleague and friend Theodora Galton for our conversations over tea and candied ginger on the use of Psalms and seals in American folk magic, and her innovative use of petition covers.

Our parishioners and clients, to whom we dedicate the work of our daily lives as we strive to serve their spiritual needs.

CANDLE MAGIC FOR THE HOME PRACTITIONER
by CATHERINE YRONWODE

Perhaps the most visible form of African American conjure at the present time is candle magic, but it is also the youngest form of rootwork, for, unlike the traditional and conservative craft of making mojos, candle magic has developed and evolved only within the past century.

A BRIEF HISTORY OF CANDLE MAGIC IN AMERICA

Oil lamps stretch back to ancient times and have long been used in both religious ceremonies and magical rites, but only after the Civil War did candles became readily available as a commercial product, sold in general stores, rather than being made at home or on the farm. By the early 20th century, paraffin candles, with a relatively high melting point compared to tallow candles and much less expensive than beeswax candles, were transported by rail nationwide — and with the invention of aniline dyes, they were soon made available in many colours.

• 1924-1940: The Song-Writer and the Folklorists

The 1924 song "Hoodoo Blues" written by New Orleans native Spencer Williams (1889-1965) and recorded by Bessie Brown contains one of the earliest mentions of candle conjure. Shortly thereafter, the systematic use of candles in African American folk magic was noticed by folklorists such as Newbell Niles Puckett, Zora Neale Hurston, and Harry Middleton Hyatt.

Puckett, writing in 1926, stated with conviction that candle magic had originated in New Orleans, where Roman Catholic candle burning combined with African-American folk magic to produce an emergent style of work.

Hurston, in the 1930s, described public candle rites such as the "pea vine drill" which took place in Spiritualist churches in New Orleans.

Hyatt interviewed practitioners all over the South from 1936 through 1940, a full ten years after Puckett, and he noted that candle magic had by then spread north to Memphis, and that Southern conjure doctors in Georgia were purchasing candle supplies from mail order houses in Memphis and Chicago. However his documentary work remained unpublished until the 1970s.

Meanwhile, in 1936, candle magic suddenly went national.

• 1936: Lewis de Claremont, Godfrey Spencer, and Mr. Young

The first printed instructions on how to dress a candle and burn it on an altar in the hoodoo manner appeared in the 1936 book "Legends of Incense, Herb, and Oil Magic" by the pseudonymous Lewis De Claremont / Louis DeClermont, who also wrote under the name Godfrey Spencer. A Jewish man, perhaps named Mr. Young, he was the owner of the Oracle Products Company in New York City, the first supply service to nationally distribute oils and candles to the African American market via mail order. His catalogue included menorahs, shofars, mezuzahs, yads, and other Jewish religious goods.

Read more about Mr. Young's candle rituals in this book:
"Legends of Incense, Herb, and Oil Magic" by Lewis De Claremont
Read a speculative biography of Mr. Young online at
LuckyMojo.com/young.html

• 1941: Mikhail Strabo and Sydney J. Rosenfeld Steiner

In a series of three booklets published from 1941-1943, the writer Mikhail Strabo described the use of candles in the Black Spiritualist churches of New York City. These ground-breaking works — "A Candle to Light Your Way," "How to Conduct a Candle Light Service," and "The Guiding Light to Power and Success" (incorporating the text of "A Candle to Light Your Way") — were sold via ads in Black-owned newspapers. They opened up a nation-wide conversation on the increasing importance of conjure work with candles.

My own research has uncovered the fact that Mikhail Strabo was a pen name of Sydney J. Rosenfeld Steiner (1894-1971), the Jewish American proprietor of Guidance House, a New York publishing company.

Steiner was a participant-observer and documentarian who respectfully verified the sources of his information. Earlier observers of candle rituals in Spiritual churches, like Zora Neale Hurston, had placed a typical folklorist's emphasis on singular incidents. Steiner, on the other hand, collaborated with an African American minister, Rev. Adele Clemens, to compile a complete manual of candle altar services, which had an enduring impact.

Read Mikhail Strabo's take on Spiritualist candle magic in this book:
"The Guiding Light to Power and Success" by Mikhail Strabo
Read a detailed biography of Sydney J. Rosenfeld Steiner online at
LuckyMojo.com/strabo.html

• 1937-1943: Rev. Adele Clemens and the Black Spiritual Churches

"How to Conduct a Candle Light Service" features an introduction by Rev. Adele Clemens, pastor of Divine Harmony Spiritual Church, which was probably located in Harlem. I have been unable to find further print or online mention of this church, but that is not unexpected, as material on the African American Spiritual Church Movement is spotty at best. Indeed the very existence of the Spiritual Church Movement and its inter-denominational umbrella organizations, such as the Colored Spiritualist Association of Churches (CSAC), remains largely unknown outside of the African American community, and has not been celebrated by the wider religious world.

This ignorance was self-imposed by European American observers. The CSAC was formed in 1922 when, in line with the institutionalized racism of the era, the National Spiritualist Association of Churches (NSAC) expelled all affiliate churches with Negro congregations. Later, when Harry Middleton Hyatt, a White Episcopalian minister, interviewed 1,600 Black rootworkers during the 1930s, he met several Spiritualist mediums with candle ministries, including a pastor who described the quadrennial CSAC convocations. However, despite this evidence, Hyatt opined that Spiritualist observances, including public candle services, were being held in "private churches."

Tantalizing glimpses of Black Spiritualism during the era of Sydney Steiner and Rev. Adele Clemens can be found in Gordon Parks' 1942 photographs of Saint Martin's Spiritual Church in Washington, D.C., as well as in the 1937 "March of Time" feature "Harlem's Black Magic." The latter is a racist and inaccurate news film which nevertheless includes clear images of signage for a number of Spiritualist churches in Harlem.

Read more about the Spiritual Church Movement in these books:
"Mules and Men" by Zora Neale Hurston
"Hoodoo Conjure Witchcraft Rootwork" by Harry Middleton Hyatt
"The Spirit of Blackhawk" by Jason Berry
"Spirit World" by Michæl Smith
"The Spiritual Churches Of New Orleans" by Claude F. Jacobs
and Andrew J. Kaslow
"Black Magic" by Yvonne Chireau
Read more about the Spiritual Church Movement online at
ReadersAndRootworkers.org/wiki/Category:Working Within the Spiritualist Tradition

• 1942: Henri Gamache and Joseph Spitalnick a.k.a. Joseph W. Kay

"The Master Book of Candle Burning" by Henri Gamache was published in 1942 and was widely advertised in black-owned newspapers like the *Chicago Defender*. It is still carried today by all the major mail-order spiritual suppliers. This work delivers exactly what it promises: detailed instructions for spiritual doctors, rootworkers, and private practitioners on "How to Burn Candles for Every Purpose," including how to select candles, anoint them, arrange them on an altar, and burn them with appropriate Biblical Psalms.

Gamache offered a unique Creole melange of Southern hoodoo, Jamaican obeah, Christianity, Jewish kabbalism, and Spiritualism. His other books are equally interesting. In particular, his "Long Lost 8th, 9th, and 10th Books of Moses" is a fascinating take on Marcus Garvey's theory that the Jewish leader Moses was a black African, "the Great Voodoo Man of the Bible."

However, Henri Gamache was a pen name, either for the Jewish American hoodoo shop owner Joe Kay (born Joseph Spitalnick; 1889-1967), who attested to the Copyright Office that he was Henri Gamache, or, according to my personal conversations with Kay's son Ed Kay, "a young college-educated Jewish woman who worked for my father and wrote books for him."

Like Sydney Steiner, "Henri Gamache," whoever he or she was, carefully and respectfully documented the work of African American Spiritual Church ministers and private practitioners, providing us with an excellent teaching manual on hoodoo candle magic.

Read more about "How to Burn Candles for Every Purpose" in this book:
"The Master Book of Candle Burning" by Henri Gamache
Read more about Henri Gamache and Joe Kay online at
LuckyMojo.com/young.html

• 1979-1980: Anna Riva and Charmaine Dey

In 1979 and 1980, hoodoo candle manuals were published by Charmaine Dey (June D. Zabawsky, 1922-1983) and Anna Riva (Dorothy Spencer, 1923-2005). Both authors blended Southern conjure and Spiritual Church customs with Gardnerian Wicca, Theosophy, and New Age beliefs.

Read more about how Neo-Paganism influenced hoodoo in these books:
"The Magic Candle" by Charmaine Dey
"Candle Burning Magic: Rituals for Good and Evil" by Anna Riva

ASSEMBLING A SET OF CANDLE MAGIC TOOLS

In order to work with lamps and candles, you will need the following tools:

- A flat, level, fireproof surface made of stone, metal, or tile.
- Metal containers such as buckets, steam-table trays, and/or bread pans.
- Saucers and bowls of brass, oven-proof glass, and white chinaware.
- A cookie sheet plus optional aluminum foil for rolling candles.
- Fireproof holders, burners, braziers, and/or ash-catchers for incense.
- Clean sand to line buckets, bowls, trays, pans, and incense pots.
- A stove or hot plate and a small pan or large spoon in which to melt wax.
- Hollow candle stands to conceal spells, metal lug-jar lids for insulation.
- Stamped metal star holders and a menorah for setting multiple candles.
- A metal candle snuffer; it can also be used as a cone-shaper for incense.
- Paper, pencils, pens, and inks for writing out petitions and prayers.
- One or more books of Solomonic or Mosaic seals, if you work with them.
- Scissors and pinking shears to trim wicks and cut out papers and seals.
- A glue stick for fixing copies of photos, seals, or art to vigil candles.
- Inscribing and carving tools: needle, nail, awl, screw-driver, or pen-knife.
- Pins and needles for sectional marking and for piercing candles.
- Kitchen tongs or a long surgical hemostat for "saving" drowning lights.
- Wooden matches, both household and fireplace size.
- Bamboo skewers for transferring flame from one candle to another.
- Tapers or lighter-candles if you dislike the use of matches or skewers.
- Saved wick-trimmings from vigil candles to use as splint-wicks.
- A mirror tile (a 3"-4" circle or square is sufficient) for reversing spells.
- Glass photo-coasters to use as covers for seals, photos, sigils, or petitions.
- Anointing oils to dress lights for a variety of spiritual conditions.
- Herbs, roots, and minerals for dressing, rolling, and/or loading candles.
- Incense, including hoodoo herbal powder incense, resins, agarbatti joss sticks, dhoop cones, and briquet incense; plus charcoal disks.
- Sachet powders for "double dressing" oiled candles and for drawing patterns such as triangles, stars, or crosses on the altar.
- Cleanup materials for wax and soot on altars, walls, and ceilings.
- A small wall-mounted home fire extinguisher.
- A Bible or Book of Psalms. The entire Book of Psalms is online here: **ReadersAndRootworkers.org/wiki/Category:The Book of Psalms**

CHOOSING YOUR LIGHTS

Lights come in many styles, sizes, and colours. You won't need all of them in your work, and in time you may come to rely on certain favourite types.

• Oil Lamps

Oil lamps have long been used around the world for light and magic. Each geographical region has its favoured lamp fuels, from Middle Eastern and Mediterranean Olive oil to South Asian clarified butter or ghee. Oil fuels themselves have symbolic meanings: Sunflower oil for health, Olive oil for blessings, Castor oil for curses, and Walnut oil for break-ups and removals.

In America, before the advent of rural electrification, Whale oil and kerosene (the latter also called coal oil or lamp oil) were the preferred fuels for rural lighting. Metal lanterns were used outdoors in the wind and rain; parlour lamps with tall glass chimneys provided illumination in the home.

When burning a kerosene lamp, always trim your wicks, keep the flame below the smoking point, and clean your chimney at least once a day. Blow kerosene lamps out by cupping your hand and going "poof" across the top of the chimney; never turn the wick down to snuff it; it won't relight well.

A vegetable oil lamp made in a canning jar does not require a chimney. Craft a simple wick for it from rolled bandage cotton because vegetable oil will not draw up through a tightly woven kerosene lamp wick. Cut or bend a simple piece of metal to hold the wick above the level of the oil. It's easy!

To fix a coal oil or vegetable oil lamp for love, money, or protection, place lucky coins, roots, minerals, or amulets in the fuel reservoir. Set name-papers, petitions, seals, or Psalms under the lamp, or hang them from a string tied around the neck of the reservoir. You may tint the oil, but it is not necessary.

The advantages of Oil Lamps:
- They burn for very, very long periods of time.
- Reservoirs can be refilled while the lamps are burning.
- They tend to be fairly safe if left unattended.

The disadvantages of Oil Lamps:
- They may give off unpleasant odours.
- They are difficult to read for divinatory purposes.

• Free-Standing Cylinder and Taper Candles

Early candles were made of beeswax or tallow (animal fat), but most are now made of paraffin (petroleum wax) or hardened vegetable oil. Because many suppliers to the African-American market in the 1940s were Jews, they naturally offered white Sabbath candles, branched menorah candle holders, and multi-coloured Hanukkah candles to their customers, imparting a festive kabbalistic glow to hoodoo altar rites which has persisted to this day. Popular sizes are 4" altar lights (chime candles), 6" offertory candles (household candles), and 9" jumbo candles in ten colours, plus gold and silver 12" tapers.

The advantages of 3", 4", 6", 9", and 12" free-standing candles:
- They are cheap, widely available, and have predictable burn times.
- They come in a wide variety of magically symbolic colours.
- They are easy to dress with oils or to roll in an herb-wax mix.

The disadvantages of 3", 4", 6", and 9", and 12" free-standing candles:
- Purchasing candle stands to hold them is an extra expense.
- They are not safe to burn unattended, although many people set them in deep metal bowls, bread pans, kitchen sinks, or bath tubs.

• Astral Candles and Candles Rolled or Fixed with Herbs

To fix free-standing candles with herbs or minerals, melt a thin layer of wax on a cookie sheet over a stove or hot-plate, sprinkle on the crumbled items, add a drop of conjure oil, remove from the heat, and roll the candle in the wax as it hardens. You can line the cookie sheet with foil to aid clean-up.

To make astral candles, select a core candle coloured for the person's sun sign, plus colours for the top and bottom of the outer wax layer — half for the ruling planet (or, if you know it, for the rising sign) and half for the moon sign. Mix in herbs appropriate to each half. See the illustration on page 15.

The advantages of astral and herb-rolled candles:
- They are satisfying to make and can be highly personalized.

The disadvantages of astral and herb-rolled candles:
- You will need equipment and spare time to make them.

• Double Action and Reversible Candles

Double action candles are 6" or 9" cylinders that are half black and half another colour — red for love, green for money, white for blessings. They send troubles back to the person who sent them and are called "double action" because they both repel jinxes and attract what is desired. These candles are "butted" before they are lit. The original tip is cut off and a new tip is cut on the black half, so the bad luck will burn off first, leaving the good luck at the end. Inscribe the enemy's name backwards in the black half and your own name normally in the coloured portion. Apply Reversing Oil to the black end, stroking away from yourself, and a second helping of Reversing Oil to the coloured half, stroking toward yourself.

Once butted, they are placed on a mirror and dusted with Reversing sachet and/or circled counter-clockwise with a ring of Crab shell powder (because "Crabs walk backward" and uncross jinxes). It is not necessary to set them according to the planetary rulerships, but folks who work that way turn back money jinxes on Thursday, love jinxes on Friday, and health jinxes on Sunday.

Another way to burn a double action candle is to carve a second tip on the black end, dress it as described above, and stick it at the mid-point onto a nail that has been driven through a board. The nail holds the candle horizontal, like a compass needle. Point the black half toward the enemy and the coloured half toward yourself. Light both ends at the same time. This is a messy burn, so use a metal pan lined with aluminum foil to confine the dripping wax.

Reversing candles, also called Reversibles, have a red core and a black outer layer. The red shows through at the tip. They are butted, dressed, and dusted as above, and burned upside down on mirrors, but all the names are inscribed backwards, in mirror writing. Reversibles can be made into rolled candles, too, using black wax dosed with Reversing Oil, Agrimony, Crab shell powder, Rue, and Aspand. Finish by rolling them in shards of mirror-glass.

The advantages of 6" and 9" double action and reversible candles:
- They are inexpensive.

The disadvantages of 6" and 9" double action and reversible candles:
- They are not safe to burn unattended.
- Butting them and carving new tips is a job of work.
- Purchasing candle stands to hold them is an extra expense.

• Figural Candles

In addition to stocking offertory candles, spiritual suppliers, as early as the 1930s, provided figural or "image" candles for special uses. More expensive than plain offertory candles, figurals are preferred by many practitioners when working unusual or extremely strong spells, because their visual symbolism is easy to see, and by carving names or other features in them, they can be personalized to represent individuals, in what amounts to a cross between working with candles and working with doll-babies or poppets.

"The Master Book of Candle Burning" by Henri Gamache was illustrated with many pictures of figural candles. (Recent reprints of the book omit these, unfortunately.) Among the figurals depicted were candles in the form of a baby-doll, a crucifix, and a Jewish high priest. Catalogue advertisements of the 1930s and 1940s showed other examples of figurals we might consider strange today: Lucky Dutch Boy and Girl candles, for instance, which were seemingly cast from porcelain figurine moulds.

By the mid-1940s, almost every order house that sold hoodoo supplies nation-wide was advertising named crucifix, 7-knob, and master hand candles. By the early 1950s, candles in the shape of the Devil and naked men and women were offered for sale. The 1960s probably saw the greatest variety of figural candles, as bride-and-groom, mummy, old witch, snake-on-pillar, and Halloween black cat figures became available.

The stock of figural candles varies greatly from one supplier to another, as the moulds for most of these candles are registered with the United States Patent and Trade Mark Office, and copying them is forbidden by law.

The advantages of figural candles:
- The images are a great aid to concentration and focus.
- They are ideal for moving candle spells.
- They can be used as doll-babies and still burned.
- They produce piles of wax for use in divination.
- They come in a variety of colours and are easily dressed with oils.

The disadvantages of figural candles:
- They are relatively expensive.
- They are more breakable than plain candles.
- They have variable and unpredictable burn times.

• The Symbolism of Figural Candles

Among the most popular figural candles are the following:

- Black Cat: Black for gamblers and risk-takers to have good luck.
- Bride-and-Groom, Bride-and-Bride, Groom-and-Groom (couple side by side): Red for passion, pink for reconciliation, white to attract new love or sanctify marriage, black for harm to a couple, blue for tranquil peace.
- Skull candle to influence another's thoughts: White for healing, red for love, green for money; black for meditation on death.
- Divorce candle (man and woman back to back): Black for a break-up.
- Lady (clothed woman) and Gentleman (clothed man) for job, school, or career: White for new encounters; pink for reconciliation or friendship; red for love; blue for health or peace on the job; black for harm.
- Adam (nude male figure) and Eve (nude female figure): White to meet someone new, pink and red for love spells, blue for peacefulness at home or to bring about faithfulness, black for harm or revenge.
- Male Member (penis) and Female Member (vulva): White for a new partner or for chastity, pink for friendly sexuality, red for passion, blue for fidelity or healing, black to control a person's sex or for sex worship.
- Cross or Crucifix candle: White for spiritual purity, black for personal power, brown for court cases, green for money, red for love, orange for change, yellow for devotion, pink for romance.
- Devil: Red for commanding lust and sex, green for collecting money owed or for gambler's luck, black for doing harm to an enemy.
- Baphomet or Sabbatic Goat: Red for lust, black for Satanic forces.
- Pyramid with Eye: Green for money drawing.
- 7-Knob Wishing Candle (flattened spheres stacked seven-high): White for healing, black to do evil, green for money spells, red for love spells. Carve a brief wish on each knob — either the same wish seven times or seven different wishes, one per knob. Burn for seven days.
- Lovers (nude couple): Red for sexual passion, white for new love.
- Master Candle (large pillar moulded to look as if a hand is holding it): In Spiritual Churches congregants' candles are lit from it, as a helper light.
- Seven Charm Sortilege Candle (hand-made candle that contains seven tiny metal charms, amulets, milagros, or ex-votos inside): Burned in sections to reveal one charm per day over the course of seven days.

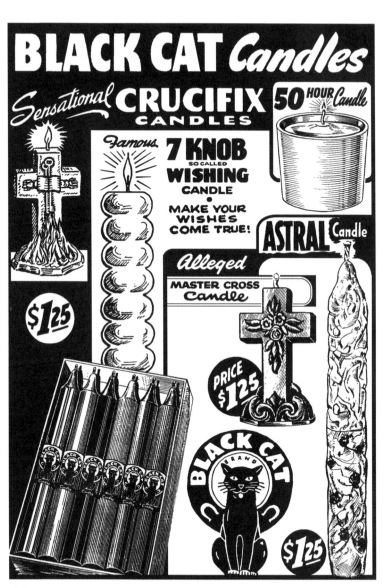

Offertory, figural, and votive candles sold by Morton Neumann's King Novelty Company during the 1930s. Art by Charles C. Dawson.

• Glass-Encased Candles

By 1945, although American mail order hoodoo catalogues primarily sold free-standing Jewish Sabbath and Hanukkah candles under brand names such as Black Cat, Success, and Master Power, they also began to carry what they called "religious," "holy," or "sanctuary" candles — glass-encased candles of various sizes bearing printed paper labels or decals depicting Catholic saints.

These glass-encased candles were popular in Catholic churches, but made little impact on conjure for the next 30 years. Most candle shops didn't carry them, probably because hoodoo practitioners are primarily Protestants.

In the mid-1970s, a wave of Latin American immigrants brought Catholic candle customs to America. At that point, enterprising companies like the Lama Temple of Chicago and Skippy's Candles of Detroit responded by designing glass-encased conjure candles, silk-screen printed with secular lucky, protective, and aggressive images. The silk-screening machines were expensive and, as a result, the entire field of imprinted religious and secular vigil candles was controlled by less than a half-dozen factories nation-wide.

In the 1990s, with the new availability of digital colour printing, suppliers across America began to design their own conjure candles with paper labels, which broke the near-monopoly on vigil candles for the hoodoo market.

In the 21st century, offertory and figural candles share shelf space in curio shops with religious and secular vigil candles. In short, a merger between hoodoo and Catholic candle burning traditions has been effected. Meanwhile, as the price of oil has risen, glass candle tubes have became narrower and a "nine day novena" or "seven day vigil light" now burns for five days at most.

The advantages of glass-encased candles:
- They are relatively safe to leave unattended.
- They leave signs of smoke and wax for divination.
- They come in a variety of colours.
- Jews like it that they don't need re-lighting on the Sabbath.

The disadvantages of glass-encased candles:
- They are heavy, and hence costly to ship.
- They sometimes break or explode while burning.
- They get very hot at the bottom as they burn out; stand them atop plain gold tin-plate metal lug-jar lids to protect fine altar surfaces.

• Religious Novena Candles

Strictly speaking, novena candles are glass-encased candles designed to be burned for nine days while Catholic votary prayers were made. Colour symbolism is not always part of Catholic candle lore, although some saints do have certain colour associations, such as green for Saint Jude and red for Saint Expedite. It is not necessary to dress novena candles with oils, although many people anoint them with Holy Oil, named saint oils, or hoodoo oils.

The use of glass-encased novena candles is widespread in Catholic Latin America, as well as in syncretic African-Caribbean religions. Beginning in the late 1970s, Cuban, Mexican, Guatemalan, and Salvadoran immigrants entered the USA in great numbers, which led to the increased marketing of novena candles here. Suddenly, not only could you find candles dedicated to well-known Catholic figures like Saint Jude, but also those featuring a host of saints previously little known here, such as San Martin Caballero (Saint Martin of Tours) and the Nino de Atocha (Infant of Atocha). Some of the new novena candles honoured Catholic folk saints and holy apparitions that are revered in Latin America but have not been officially approved by the Vatican, like the Anima Sola (Lonely Soul), a Mexican favourite; the Seven African Powers (Siete Potencias), a staple image representing Cuban Santeria's mingling of Catholic saints with the West African orishas, and the syncretic Catholic Mayan patron deity of Guatemala known as Maximon or San Simon.

Technical advances in colour printing have also led to the development of religious candles for other faiths. For instance, starting in the 1990s, i myself put into production a line of Hindu religious candles, a line of Jewish Archangel candles, and lines for Zodiac signs and the Planets. Candle makers now find it easy to design and carry a Mayan item such as the Chuparrosa love candle; a Pagan line with special colours and designs for Norse, Celtic, or Classical deities; and a Kemetic line to honour the ancient Egyptian gods.

The advantages of glass-encased religious novena candles:
   • The same as other glass-encased candles.

The disadvantages of glass-encased religious novena candles:
   • The same as other glass-encased candles.
   • Religious adherence, proof of initiation, and other restrictions may be part of the proper or approved use of religious candles.

• Secular and Magical Vigil Lights

The text and images found on hoodoo vigil candles are typically the same as those used in hoodoo formulæ for anointing oils, with names such as Fast Luck, Uncrossing, Compelling, Money House Blessing, and the like. Old ways of dressing free-standing and figural candles with anointing oils and herbs have been modified considerably to accommodate the use of vigil candles. Since the sides of a glass-encased candle cannot be rubbed with oil, it is customary for the retailer rather than the user to dress the light. This can be done by poking holes or inscribing names in the wax with a nail, awl, or knife, dripping in an appropriate anointing oil, adding herbs, and finishing off the top with symbolically coloured glitter. This technique leaves the customer in danger of spilling the dressing oil while carrying the candle home, so in many stores the dressed candle is covered with a plastic sandwich bag or cling wrap, held in place by a rubber band.

Vigil candles also necessitate modifications in old-style spells designed to be worked over a length of time. The old pin or needle measuring technique for burning candles in sections cannot be employed on glass-encased candles, so timed burning or measuring the glass into sections with a marking-pen has taken its place. These newer methods weaken the practitioner's involvement in the spell, however, because there are no pins or needles left over to make the crosses and double crosses prescribed in the older workings. A glass-encased candle spell therefore takes on a slightly "ritual" or "religious" tone, in that one's prayers, desires, or wishes are expected to do the work alone, as contrasted to an offertory or figural candle spell, in which the manipulation of magical objects — candle, flame, paper, herbs, and needles or pins — is integral to doing the job.

The advantages of glass-encased secular and magical vigil candles:
  • The same as other glass-encased candles.

The disadvantages of glass-encased secular and magical vigil candles:
  • The same as other glass-encased candles.
  • Proprietary brand names for vigil lights have proliferated to the point of causing confusion among users: "What's the difference between Crown of Success candles and Pinnacle of Success candles, and which one is best?" is not an uncommon question.

• Unlabelled Plain Glass-Encased Candles

Unlabelled glass-encased candles, often called "plain" lights, are popular with those who don't want family members or visitors to know their business. Fixed with herbs and oils, they can be introduced into the home under the name of "mood lighting" or "holy lights." Their actual purposes — and the oils used to dress them — remain the secret of the one who lights them. Custom labels made with photos, tarot card images, Solomonic or Mosaic seals, or personal sigils can be glued onto plain vigils. Alternatively, the glass may be painted and designs scratched through to reveal the colour of the wax.

The advantages of glass-encased unlabelled or plain candles:
  • The same as other glass-encased candles.
  • Secrecy and discretion are assured if they remain unlabelled.
  • Labels can be added, using art, photos, tarot cards, seals, or paint.

The disadvantages of glass-encased unlabelled or plain candles:
  • The same as other glass-encased candles.

• Multi-Layer Glass-Encased Candles

The most popular multi-colour glass-encased vigil light is the black-on-red Reversing candle to return evil to the sender — a modification of the double action candle. Be sure to get the variety with black on top and red beneath, otherwise you will be burning off your luck and end up left with your curses. Another two-layer vigil light is the gold-and-green, used for job-getting and business prosperity. Brand names include Lady Luck and Prosperity. Seven-layer candles poured with wax in varied hues include the Lucky Prophet Lafin Buddha Brand All Purpose Novena Candle that grants "7 desires" like a 7-knob candle; the seven-layer Planet brand candle for astrological use; and the Seven African Powers candle of Santeria.

The advantages of glass-encased multi-layer candles:
  • The same as other glass-encased candles.

The disadvantages of glass-encased multi-layer candles:
  • The same as other glass-encased candles.

• Pull-Out Candle Refills for Glass-Encased Candles

Pull-out candles are hard-wax refills for novena and vigil light glasses:

The advantages of pull-out candles:
- • Pull-outs are real wax, not the gooey semi-solid found in glass-encased lights; they are sturdy enough to burn as stand-alones.
- • They can be inscribed, loaded with personal concerns or petitions, and dressed with oil before insertion into the glass holder.
- • Favourite glass holders can be re-used again and again.

The disadvantages of pull-out candles:
- • At 2" by 7", they do not fit into every brand of candle glass.
- • Due to the high quality of their wax, the cost per pull-out candle is almost the same as the cost of a new glass-encased candle.

• Votive Candles and Stubbies

Properly speaking, any candle burned as the prelude to or the result of a spiritual vow is a votive candle, but although votive candles are defined by their function, not their form, in the United States, we generally refer to encased candles under 2" in height as tea lights, those from 2"-5" in height as votive candles, and those in cylinders taller than 7" as glass-encased candles.

Votives are made in two ways — either poured into holders or free-standing. The latter, which are essentially just short pull-outs, are called "stubbies." Votives burn for 10-15 hours in a holder. White stubbies may be placed inside coloured glass holders of various hues and will shine with the symbolic colours of their holders. Stubbies burned as free-standing candles have a shorter burn time, but they often yield useful melted wax divinations.

The advantages of votive candles:
- • They are relatively safe to burn unattended in holders.
- • Dressed white votives can be burned in coloured glass holders.

The disadvantages of votive candles:
- • Glass holders may break unexpectedly.
- • If burned in holders, they may leave few or no divination signs.

• Lux Perpetua Candles

Lux perpetua ("eternal light") candles originate in Latin America. They are comprised of sticky-soft wax that may also contain animal fat, poured into stiff paper cups or cylinders printed with Catholic devotionary images.

The advantages of lux perpetua candles:
  • They are very pretty and highly folkloric.

The disadvantages of lux perpetua candles:
  • The paper containers may catch fire.

• Tea Lights

Tea lights are small candles poured into aluminum cups. Designed for use at the table to keep foods and drinks warm (hence the name "tea light"), they make great refills for glass votive candle holders.

The advantages of tea lights:
  • They are cheap and they burn quickly, reducing attendance time.

The disadvantages of tea lights:
  • They burn so completely that they leave no divination signs.

• Re-Made Candles

You can re-use clean wax to make new candles. Sort hard wax by colour and melt it to use as a coating for herb-rolled or astral candles, or dye it black for dipping double action candles. If you burn vigil lights, recycle the glass, but save one back. If a vigil breaks, melt the soft wax, fish out the wick and metal wick-holder, set them in the empty glass, and pour in the salvaged wax.

The advantages of re-made candles:
  • They are inexpensive and satisfying to make.

The disadvantages of re-made candles:
  • You will need equipment and spare time to make them.

ALTAR LAYOUTS FOR LAMP AND CANDLE SPELLS

Once you have chosen your light, you have the option of choosing a way of working at your altar, such as fixing spiritual lamps, casting moving candle spells, setting vigils or novena candles, and burning in runs.

• Lamp Spells

After being fixed with curios and roots, lamps are prayed over, set on top of name-papers, seals, or Psalms, or have petitions attached to them and you then select an appropriate time for the ceremonial lighting. Final prayers or petitions are made over the lamps as they are lit and set to work.

Lamps are versatile and can be used in several ways. First, because of their long burn time and the fact that they can be refilled while burning, some folks choose lamps for long-term spells regarding health, business, family matters, and justice cases. Other practitioners dedicate several lamps to specific conditions, such as love, money, or health, and then either burn them "as needed" or use them as helper lights while working short-term candle spells.

• Fixed Candle Spells

A fixed candle spell involves the use of any type of candle that, once dressed and prepared, is left to burn in place without being moved.

To fix a candle, it may be named for a client or a target individual; carved with words, symbols, or sigils; loaded with personal concerns like hair or fingernail clippings; and anointed, dressed, or blessed with condition oils and herbs, roots, and minerals appropriate to the work. Sachet powders suitable to the condition may be dusted on it, or it may be sprinkled with glitter to reflect wishes out into the universe many times over.

Depending on the nature of the work, a fixed candle may be burned in sections — either a segment at a time or for a specific time-span per session — or it may be burned straight through, with or without the recitation of Psalms. If it is to be burned in one sitting, the practitioner may time the work so that the light burns in concert with natural occurrences like sunrise and sunset or so that it stays alight and provides illumination during the casting of a further spell, such as a ritual of spiritual bathing and cleansing or the creation of a mojo bag, doll-baby, talisman, or container spell.

• Setting Lights

Setting lights is a term used when working for a desired outcome by placing name papers, photos, petitions, Psalms, and/or Solomonic or Mosaic seals under a light and letting it burn through until it is completely finished. The papers may be loose or folded into packets. They may be laid flat on the altar or protected by an overturned saucer or a glass photo-coaster cover. They may be wrapped around the candle's butt end in the holder or placed inside the bottom of a hollow candle-stand. In all cases, the papers are said to be "set" under the candle in the same way that eggs are set under a broody hen. Both fixed or unfixed lights can be set, but the former is the more common practice. Lights suitable for setting include oil lamps, figurals, votives, pillars, jumbos, glass-encased candles, or a "sacred octave" of offertory candles lit daily for eight days. The last-named may be an adaption of the traditional eight-day Jewish Hanukkah celebration to the practice of hoodoo; it is fully described in Mikhail Strabo's "The Guiding Light to Power and Success."

• Moving Candle Spells

Moving candle spells are progressive workings in which the candles are repositioned during the course of being burned, essentially acting out the intentions of the spell-caster. The candle wax colours chosen for moving candle spells generally relate to the condition for which the spell is being cast, the roles of the people involved, or their zodiacal signs. Candle forms used in these spells include offertory, jumbo, pillar, double action, reversible, seven-knob, figural, or votive candles and they may be accompanied by secondary helper lights, such as astral candles, vigil lights, or oil lamps.

To separate or break up a couple, to move an unwanted neighbour or enemy off, to send a troublesome co-worker away, or to drive customers away from a store, we fix and dress a candle for each person or class of persons, face the two candles away from one another, and burn them in sections, moving them apart over the course of several days.

To bring about a reconciliation in love, to effect a renewal of friendship, to get a job offer, to bring a new co-worker into a job-site, or to increase customer flow into a business, we position the prepared candles facing one another and burn them in sections, slowly bringing them closer and closer until, at the end of several days, they are touching one another on the altar.

• Helper Lights

The hoodoo term "helper light" is a literal English translation of the Hebrew "shamash" — the "helper light" from which the eight traditional lamps or candles of Hanukkah are lit. In conjure work, helper lights are used as lighter candles and also to sustain moving candle spells over the course of several days by remaining lit on the altar between scheduled burning sessions.

• Burning Candles in Sections

To burn a candle "in sections" has several meanings. In some spells, the candle is burned a half-inch at a time for several days. In other spells, it is burned at timed intervals, such as 15 minutes at each sunrise and sunset, It may be lit at specified hours, such as 9:00 in the morning and 9:00 at night. It may be burned on certain days, such as every Saturday for revenge, or every Monday, Wednesday, and Friday for good works. It may be burned over a specified number of days — three, seven, or nine being typical choices.

When a candle is burned in sections, it is not blown out at the end of each session, but rather pinched or snuffed out, to signify that the spell is not yet complete. A more graceful way to put out candles than by spitting on your fingers and pinching them out is to snuff them with a candle snuffer. This also reduces objectionable smoke from the snuffed candle. Decorative metal snuffers make elegant altar tools for those who burn candles in sections.

• The Candle Divided by Seven Needles or Pins

This may be the oldest form of the seven-day candle. To make one, poke seven needles into a candle, dividing it into seven parts. The seventh needle or pin can go at the top or at the bottom, but no one i know ever uses SIX needles or pins to divide the candle into seven parts. Dress the candle, set a petition paper under it and burn it for seven nights, pinching or snuffing it out each time a needle falls. Save the needles as they fall, and when the work is done, stick them into the paper in the form of two "x" patterns surrounding a double-cross made of two horizontals and an upright: X ‡ X. Wrap and sew the paper in leather and carry it as a mojo hand for luck. Bury it under your doorstep for protection or to draw love or money. To get rid of something or someone, throw it away into a crossroads, running water, or a graveyard.

• Burning Candles in a Triangle, Square, Cross, Star, or Circle

Within the conjure community, the term "burning candles in a triangle" has developed two different meanings. Both terms are quite traditional but they refer to two entirely different methods. "Burning candles in a triangle" originally referred to candles set on three-cornered papers. In his influential 1936 book, "Legends of Incense, Herb, and Oil Magic," Lewis De Claremont described how to draw an upward-pointing triangle for blessings or a downward-pointing one for curses, and how to set a dressed light on it. His European grimoire methods, which also included the use of Mosaic seals and talismans, proved to be very popular in hoodoo.

De Claremont further taught that when blessed offertory candles were distributed in church to be saved for private use at a later date, one could draw a triangle on cloth or paper, anoint it with Bible Oil, and wrap the candle in it, "to keep it free from the contamination of the vibrations of others."

An entirely different form of "burning candles in a triangle" is that which is achieved by arraying three candles around a central object. Depending on your intentions, the candles may all be the same colour, or each one may be different in colour. A line of sachet powders or herbal incense powders on the altar may define the triangle. In the center is the focal object of the spell, such as a figural candle, a vigil candle, a doll-baby, a mojo hand, a statuary figure, an easel-framed photo, or a piece of amuletic jewelry.

This method is often elaborated to include four candles in a square or cross, six candles in a hexagonal star, or eight candles in an octagonal star. Other patterns include a multi-pointed crown, a circle, and so forth.

• Burning Candles on a Seal, Sigil, or Psalm

Those who work with the Psalms, Solomonic or Mosaic seals, or hand-drawn sigils often set candles on them, after the manner of setting candles on name-papers or petitions. Some practitioners prefer to make photocopies of the Psalms, seals, or sigils, or to purchase seals pre-printed on parchment paper, while others enjoy writing and drawing the words or images by hand.

A seal, sigil, or Psalm can be preserved for future use by placing it inside a glass photo-coaster cover of the type commonly used as wedding souvenirs. A permanent cover of this type containing, for instance, a Seal of Venus or Jupiter, can be placed over successive individual petitions for love or money.

CANDLES BY COLOUR

In the old days, most candles were white or tan, but our modern candle colours link into a symbol-system influenced by European magical traditions:

• Colour Symbolism in Candles

- Red — love, sexuality, affection, passion, reunion, bodily vigour.
- Orange — change of plans, opening the way, prophetic dreams.
- Yellow — devotion, prayer, money (gold), cheer, attraction, success.
- Green — money, gambling luck, business, a good job, abundant crops.
- Blue — peace, harmony, joy, kindly intentions, healing, spirituality.
- Purple — mastery, power, ambition, control, command.
- Pink — attraction, romance, clean living, friendship, optimism, success.
- Brown — court cases, mediations, neutrality, animals, lost articles.
- Black — repulsion, dark thoughts, sorrow, evil, and freedom from evil.
- White — spiritual blessings, purity, healing, rest; the "universal" colour.
- Red and black double action — to send back a love-jinxing spell.
- White and black double action — to return all evil to the sender.
- Green and black double action — to send back a money-jinxing spell.

INCENSE ON THE ALTAR

Experienced workers often accompany candle work with the burning of incense. Herb-based powder incense formed into cones, resin incense burned on charcoal, agarbatti joss sticks, dhoop, and briquet incense are all popular.

• The Use of Incense on the Candle or Lamp Altar

Some folks light altar incense to set the mood as they inscribe, dress and light their candles. Others believe that the lighting of the candles must come first, with incense following. Try it both ways; the choice is yours.

If you have no herbs on hand to dress a candle, a pinch of appropriate powder incense made with herbs and resins will serve very well. Incense powder can also be used like sachet powder to draw patterns on the altar.

Joss stick incense can be lodged in the socket of the same holder as a free-standing candle. Three sticks surrounding a single light gives a nice effect.

THE BEST TIME FOR YOUR CANDLE SPELL

When i am asked how to pick the "best time" to cast a spell, i always reply that while many good conjure doctors set their lights "by need" and never bother with timing, an equal number of traditional workers do utilize various forms of timing — and here is an outline of some of our favourite systems.

• Timing Your Candle or Lamp Work by the Time of Day

The time of day to start a light may be related to the goal of the work. Some spells call for candles or lamps at sunrise and sunset, or every morning, noon and night. Others specify midnight, the traditional "witching hour."

To draw in good influences, you may work in the morning, as the sun rises, or when both clock hands are rising, for instance, in the second half of the hours between six and twelve — or a combination of these ideas.

To repel or cast off influences, you may work in the evening, as the sun goes down, or when both hands on the clock are falling, in the first half of the hours from twelve to six — or you may combine these two ideas.

• Timing Your Candle or Lamp Work by the Planets

You may work in accord with the planets that rule the days of the week:

- Sunday: The Sun (Sol, Apollo) is for fatherhood, men and boys, blessing, health and healing, success, fame, and will power.
- Monday: The Moon (Luna, Selene, Diana, Artemis) is for motherhood, women and girls, home, family, dreams, visions, night, and water.
- Tuesday: Mars (Ares, Twi) is for strength, athleticism, competition, conflict, confrontation, war, courage, risk-taking, victory, and blood.
- Wednesday: Mercury (Wotan, Hermes) is for communication, verbal skills, messages, trickery, gambling, speech, and broadcasting.
- Thursday: Jupiter (Thor, Zeus), is for expansion, wealth, patronage, money (Europe), power, dignified rulership, and royalty.
- Friday: Venus (Freya, Aphrodite) is for love, pleasure, sexuality, artistry, seduction, æsthetics, plants, æsthetic beauty, and money.
- Saturday: Saturn (Saturnus, Chronos) is for agriculture, duty, enemies, curses, death, and restrictions or limitations on the works of others.

• Timing Your Candle or Lamp Work by the Phase of the Moon

The waxing moon is employed by many for spells of increase and gain, while the waning moon is utilized for spells of decrease or loss.
See the current Moon phase online here:
LuckyMojo.com/moonphases.html

• Timing Your Candle or Lamp Work by the Sign of the Moon

Planting guides like "The Farmer's Almanac" give the moon's sign for every day of the year. Each sign rules certain areas of life, and as the moon traverses the signs, its energy may help or hinder a spell begun in that sign.

- Aries The Ram: Cardinal Fire, ruled by Mars. Creative, energetic, adaptable, and insightful. The head, brain, eyes, and face.
- Taurus The Bull: Fixed Earth, ruled by Venus. Strong, steady, sensual, and stubborn. The neck, throat, and thyroid.
- Gemini The Twins: Mutable Air, ruled by Mercury. Intelligent, inconstant, and verbal. The lungs, shoulders, arms, hands, and nerves.
- Cancer The Crab: Cardinal Water, ruled by The Moon. Sensitive, home-loving, quiet, and defensive. The breasts and the stomach.
- Leo The Lion: Fixed Fire, ruled by The Sun. Noble, showy, egoistic, and generous. The heart and the spine.
- Virgo The Virgin: Mutable Earth, ruled by Mercury. Modest, precise, accurate, and analytical. The intestines and the spleen.
- Libra The Scales: Cardinal Air, ruled by Venus. Balanced, diplomatic, indecisive, and æsthetic. The kidneys and the skin.
- Scorpio The Scorpion: Fixed Water, ruled by Mars and Pluto. Deep, determined, sexual, and skeptical. The genitals and the rectum.
- Sagittarius The Archer: Mutable Fire, ruled by Jupiter. Philosophical, adventurous, uncommitted. The hips, thighs, liver, and sciatic nerve.
- Capricorn The Sea-Goat: Cardinal Earth, ruled by Saturn. Capable, disciplined, reliable, uncompromising. The knees, joints, and bones.
- Aquarius The Water-Bearer: Fixed Air, ruled by Saturn and Urania. Scientific, humanitarian, and unconventional. The calves and ankles.
- Pisces The Fishes: Mutable Water, ruled by Jupiter and Neptune. Mystical, empathetic, and poetic. The feet and the immune system.

HOW TO PREPARE A CANDLE FOR USE

• Inscribing, Carving, Butting, and Loading Your Candle

Candles are inscribed by writing a name, command, symbol, or sigil in the wax with a pin, needle, nail, awl, or knife-point to indicate on whose behalf they are being burned or to dedicate them to a particular intention. On free-standing candles, write the name in spirals, like the stripes on a barber pole. On figurals the name goes at the base or down the back.

Carving a candle modifies it in a sculptural sense. Offertory and jumbo candles can be carved to resemble figures, and figural candles are modified through carving to emphasize, deform, or destroy certain aspects of the figure they represent, depending on the purpose of the spell.

Butting a light is a form of carving a free-standing candle in which the original tip is cut off and a new tip is carved at the butt-end.

A candle may be loaded by digging a hole or pit, usually at the bottom, inserting personal concerns, papers, and/or herbs into a hole, melting the dug-out wax in a large spoon, and pouring it back in the hole to seal it.

• Anointing or Dressing Your Candle

Dress your candle with an appropriate anointing oil or a combination of two or more oils. These usually come in 1/2 oz. bottles, so if you have a large practice or a candle ministry, order the 4 oz. custom blends that suppliers offer as Rootworkers and Church Specials, or use all-purpose Special Oil No. 20.

- Dress free-standing candles upward to draw and downward to repel or dress them both ways from the middle to "magnetize" them.
- Dress double action candles both ways from the middle.
- Dress figural candles as if they were the figure they represent.
- Try the old-school method of sprinkling oiled candles with sachet powders or crushed herbs selected for their specific spiritual powers.
- Dress glass-encased candles by poking holes or engraving a name or symbol in the wax, then drizzling in a few drops of oil. Top with herbs and glitter, but use care; too much oil will drown the wick and too many herbs may lead to the entire top surface catching on fire, a hazard that may also result in a black, sooty burn and a negative candle divination.

• Praying Over and Sealing or Knocking Your Candle

Your candle should be prayed over and sealed or knocked to fix it.

You may pray in your own words or by recitation of the Psalms or scriptures, or you may combine the two. If you are praying over many candles at once, cover them with a white prayer cloth and treat them as one unit.

There are several ways to seal a candle. You may lay hands on it, lift it up and tap the bottom three times on the altar, knock it three times on the top with your fist, or hold it up and recite a prayer over it, such as, *"From my heart to God's heart* (hold it to your breast, then move it up and outward), *from my mouth to God's ear* (kiss it, then hold it up and outward), *from my mind to the mind of God* (touch it to your forehead, then turn it up and outward)."* You may also tap or knock the altar three times instead of tapping the candle. You can combine these techniques, for instance tapping, knocking, and tapping the candle (resulting in nine taps) or praying over and laying hands on the candle, and then tapping the altar three times.

• Preparing a Petition or Name-Paper for Your Candle or Lamp

It is common practice to write out a petition and/or a name on paper and to place the paper beneath the candle or lamp, sometimes under an overturned saucer to protect it from burning. The type of paper used is variable, but many favour brown paper neatly torn from a grocery sack. If a photo is used, it is customary to write the name and birth date on the back.

When a name-paper is placed under a candle, this is called "burning a candle on [him or her]" — and it can be done for love, revenge, harm, or any desired result. The earliest printed version of this spell i know dates back to 1924, in the song "Hoodoo Blues" written by the New Orleans native Spencer Williams (1889-1965) and recorded by Bessie Brown. A black Cat bone is used to return the narrator's lover and a candle is set on the enemy's picture:

Goin' 'neath her window, gonna lay a black Cat bone,
Goin' 'neath her window, gonna lay a black Cat bone,
Burn a candle on her picture, she won't let my good man alone.

For more on how to make and use papers in candle magic, see the book: **"Paper in My Shoe" by catherine yronwode**

• Lighting Your Candle or Lamp

Light each candle or lamp with a prayer. You may have prayed when fixing them, but pray again when lighting them. Use wooden matches, as they burn longer than paper ones. If you dislike the smell of matches or feel that their unpredictable burns break the flow of your movements, use a helper light or light a taper in another room, bring it to the altar, and snuff it in sand after use.

• The Order In Which Candles Are Lit

The order of lighting candles on an altar varies by practitioner. Just for a simple four-candle layout, i've seen all of the following: <>, +, x, and z.

- East, South, West, North (<>)
- North, South, East, West (+)
- Back, front, left, right (+)
- Back left, front right, back right, front left (x)
- Back left, back right, front left, front right (z)

• What To Do With Your Petition Paper At the End of the Rite

If you are burning a free-standing candle, setting the petition paper alight at the end is a great conclusion to the rite. You'll need a brass dish on the altar in which to drop the burning paper, lest you scorch your fingers. The ashes from the burnt paper can be mixed with sachet powder and used to further the spell, according to the many ways in which powders are employed.

However, if you have set a vigil light and wish to perform wax or smoke reading on the glass, igniting your paper inside the candle tube will smoke the glass and change the signs you would have seen had you left the glass alone. A clear, clean glass portends success, so it seems counter-productive to smoke up a clear glass at the end of the rite, by tossing the paper into the flame.

In such cases you may find it a better idea to save your name-paper or petition for further use than to dispose of it in flame. You may, for instance, wish to wear it in your shoe, carry it in your wallet, hide it over a door-frame, set it loose in running water, or retain it for a continuation of the candle rite at a future date. Glass photo-coaster covers are a nice way to protect petitions, Psalms, seals, and photographs that you wish to set under subsequent candles.

• How to Burn Candles in Secret

Lots of folks don't have full privacy to do spell-casting in their homes. They may live with their parents, or in shared housing such as a dormitory, or — tough as it is — they may be performing a spell that is intended to directly affect a family member in the home, such as a spouse, child, or in-law. Almost every system of magical working can be adapted to function under conditions of secrecy, but candle burning is the most difficult form of rootwork or conjure to hide, for obvious reasons.

One way to conceal candle work is to burn the candles in sections and hide them between burnings. Set them for at least 15 minutes at each session — just long enough to get them going well and to spend some time over them in prayer or petition before putting them out. In order to keep their link to the candles continuously strong during the switches from "on" time to "off" time, practitioners long ago developed two further traditions, "pinching them out" (for all candles) and "wrapping them up" (for candles that are hidden away).

In hoodoo, one oft-heard piece of advice is, "You should never blow a candle out if you want to return to it, because that ends the spell, but if you pinch it out, you can come back to it any time." This is a customary, but not compulsory, way to deal with candles that are to be burned in sections. Just lick your thumb and first finger and — sffft! — put out the wick. Or, you can keep a pretty metal candle snuffer at the altar (and it can do double-duty as a shaper for incense cones). Pinching or snuffing out the light is done for all candles burned in sections — that is, both for candles that will be left on the altar and for those that will be hidden away.

When hiding away candles or any other altar objects, it is the custom to wrap and tie them. This secures their spiritual energy, and marks them as still being in use. Wrap small candles that are being burned in sections in a triangle of paper. Place larger candles, especially vigils, in a brown paper grocery bag and twist the top shut. Candles may also be rolled up in a flat piece of brown grocery bag paper and tied with cotton packaging twine.

Another way to burn candles in secret is to have spiritual practitioners, such as those at Missionary Independent Spiritual Church, set lights for you. Church candle servers are highly discreet, but you will enjoy hoodoo candle magic more and learn to become a sharper conjure practitioner if you try casting a few candle spells on your own. If you are new to the work, start by following some simple pre-written spells, and then design your own.

CANDLE AND LAMP SPELLS FOR ALL OCCASIONS

If you want a library of candle spells, i recommend the following books:
• **"The Master Book of Candle Burning" by Henri Gamache**
• **"The Guiding Light to Power and Success" by Mikhail Strabo**
• **"The Magic Candle" by Charmaine Dey**
• **"Candle Burning Magic: Rituals for Good and Evil" by Anna Riva**
In addition, i'd also like to share some of my own personal favourites.

A WHITE CANDLE LOVE SPELL TO ATTRACT NEW LOVE

Here is a white candle love spell i was taught by a friend, Miriam Singer, who had it from another woman many years ago. It was given to me as a "woman's spell," possibly because of the phallic shape of the candle, but since i first posted it on the web in 1994, i have heard from a number of men who have used it with success and satisfaction.

Get a white candle that will burn down in due time. You will have to inscribe it, so it should be bigger than a birthday candle, and you will also have to watch it burn down to nothing, so it should not be a 24 hour votive light. A white 4" altar light or bride-and-groom candle will be just right.

Prepare an altar and decorate it with those things precious to you and to the one you love. Using a Rose thorn from a white Rose bush, inscribe the words "All my love come to me" three times on the candle. Place the inscribed candle in the center of the altar and light it. For the entire time the candle burns, gaze upon it and visualize your love coming to you in nakedness and beauty. When the candle burns out, collect the wax puddle that remains, wrap it up with the mementos from the altar and keep it in a safe place.

The result of this spell will not be "zombie" or "victim" thrall-love; but you will receive ALL the love that person has for you — which may be less than, as much as, or more than the love you have for him. Accept the degree of love you receive with grace and tenderness.

If at some future time you no longer wish to receive that person's love, dispose of the ritual remains in a simple ceremonial way. Depending on your mood, the wax puddle can be burned on a fire, buried at a crossroads, thrown into running water, mailed to him, ground to shavings and baked into a cake — or whatever you feel is appropriate. But it is your responsibility to dispose of it if you no longer want to be loved in any degree by that person.

LODESTONES AND RED CANDLE TO ATTRACT NEW LOVE

This hoodoo conjuration is a little more forceful than the white candle love spell given above. It takes seven days to complete. To perform the work, you will need a pair of large lodestones (male and female if you are heterosexual; both male or both female if you are homosexual), a packet of magnetic sand, a tray or plate (not made of steel or iron), anointing oil, small personal items or paper and ink, and a red candle. A plain offertory candle will do, but the red lovers or red bride-and-groom figural candles are particularly appropriate for drawing a partner of the opposite sex.

Before you begin lodestone love spells, determine which ends of the lodestones draw to each other most strongly. Place the lodestones on the tray, some distance apart, with the attracting ends facing each other. Behind them and between them, forming a triangle, set up the candle.

Next, name the lodestones: one for you and one for the person you wish to attract. If you can get anything of the person's (a photo, a lock of hair, nail parings), place it beneath the person's lodestone. Place something similar of yours beneath your lodestone. If you cannot get such items, write the person's name three times in red ink on one piece of paper and your name three times in red ink on another piece of paper and place those beneath the respective lodestones. If you are already having sexual relations with the person, simply anoint the lodestones with sexual fluids: semen for a "he" stone and vaginal fluids or menstrual blood for a "she" stone.

On the first day, dress the candle with a love-drawing oil, such as Come to Me, Love Me, Follow Me Boy, or Lavender Love Drops. Sprinkle a little of the oil on each lodestone as well. Light the candle and feed the lodestones with one-seventh of the magnetic sand. Concentrate on your desires. You may also read aloud the Song of Solomon, which is in the Bible. Let the candle burn one-seventh of the way down and snuff it.

The next day, move the lodestones a little closer to each other. Again light the candle and feed the lodestones with one-seventh of the magnetic sand. Concentrate on your desires and read aloud the Song of Solomon. Let the candle burn one-seventh of the way down and snuff it.

Continue in this way for seven days until the candle is finished and the lodestones are touching and are well covered with magnetic sand.

When the ritual is done, place the lodestones, still on their tray, in a safe place where they can continue to draw to each other.

COMMANDING RESPECT AT A MEETING WITH SUPERIORS

Assemble any paperwork, documentation, writing tablets, or things you will carry in to your meeting with the executive, manager, or boss.

Fix a purple or yellow candle with Commanding Oil, writing the name of the executive, manager, or boss in the wax with a needle and crossing it with your command. Prepare a paper with the name (and photo, if you can get it) of the person and your command for respect or for your proposal to be granted written over it. Put the paper under a saucer under the candle.

Light the candle and, working only by its light, dress your assembled items and the clothes and jewelry you will wear to the meeting, with Commanding Sachet Powders, Incense, Oil, or Bath Crystals dissolved in water, as is appropriate to whatever the items are made from. As you do this, recite Psalms 5, for finding favour with authorities or superiors in business.

When the work is complete, snuff out the candle and go to sleep.

In the morning, relight the candle and recite Psalms 5 again. Dress in the prepared clothes and jewelry, take the name-paper out from under the candle, and write Psalms 5 all over it in your own handwriting. Place the paper in the shoe of your dominant foot. Add a pinch of salt for protection, sugar to sweeten the person, cinnamon powder for money, John the Conqueror Root for willpower, and Gravel Root, for favour on the job.

If you have a safe place to keep the candle burning while you are at the meeting, do so. A bathtub, fireplace, or kitchen sink is generally safe, if no curtains can blow into the area and no pets can upset the candle. The candle will back you up while you are at the meeting.

Walk into the meeting carrying your dressed and prepared materials, stepping on the name of the executive, commanding him to do as you wish.

A FIXED MONEY LAMP TO BRING IN WEALTH

Place a coin of each denomination (cent, nickel, dime, etc.) plus a piece of Lodestone and a chunk of Pyrite in the reservoir of a vegetable oil or kerosene lamp, praying the 23rd Psalm over each item. Tie a rabbit foot charm onto a string and fasten it around the neck of the glass, for luck. Do the same with an old key, to open doors. Tie on a dried Wishbone, so dreams come true. Clean the chimney daily, refill the lamp by unscrewing the burner so it never goes out, and let it light your way to good fortune.

TO MAKE TWO PEOPLE FIGHT LIKE CATS AND DOGS

Get two black human-figure candles, inscribe each person's name on his or her candle with a coffin nail, dress them both with Hot Foot Oil and sprinkle Catnip on one and Dog Grass on the other, so they fight like Cats and Dogs. Burn the candles for seven days, moving them farther apart each day.

HOUSE BLESSING FOR MONEY AND PEACE IN THE HOME

Fix a blue offertory candle with House Blessing Oil and set it in a holder on top of a paper on which you have written the name of everyone in the household, crossed by the entire text of the 23rd Psalm of the Bible. Place four coins, all of the same denomination, around the candle in the form of an equal-armed cross or five-spot pattern, oriented North, South, East, and West. Light the candle and recite the 23rd Psalm aloud. As the candle finishes, burn the paper in its flame and save the ash. Bury the coins at the outside four corners of the house and bury the candle wax and ash under the house, forming a five-spot pattern to fix the spell in place. If the house is built in such a way that you cannot get under it, the wax may be buried at the front door instead.

A SKULL CANDLE TO INFLUENCE THEIR THOUGHTS

Skull candles are used to get inside peoples' minds, to influence their thoughts for good or ill. Select a skull of appropriate colour, or use white, the universal colour. Choose a symbolic weekday to start. Wait until you think the person is asleep. With a knife, hollow out a "divot" at the bottom of the candle. Load in your petition and herbs appropriate to the job. Melt the wax in a spoon and pour as much of it as you can back in, to seal the candle.

If your intent is loving, wash the candle with perfume and dress it with an appropriate oil, and then hold it in your hands as you talk to it in hypnotic and convincing tones. Do this for seven nights, and on the eighth night light it.

If your intent is coercive, heat up sewing pins, one at a time, using a long-handled hemostat, and plunge them into the skull, starting with the eyes, so they can't see your work, the ears, so they can't hear your work, the nostrils, so they can't smell your work, and the mouth, so they can't speak of your work. Then curse the skull as you insert pins all over, a few at a time, for seven nights. On the eighth night, pour your coercive oil over it and light it.

GREEN CANDLE JOB-GETTING OR WAGE INCREASE SPELL

Represent yourself by a white clothed lady or gentleman candle. Inscribe it with your name and dress it with Attraction Oil and Crown of Success Oil. Represent a new job with a green 7-knob candle. Inscribe seven wishes on the 7 knobs and dress it with a blend of Steady Work Oil and Attraction Oil. Represent a pay raise with a green pyramid candle. Inscribe your petition on it and dress it with a blend of Attraction Oil, Pay Me Oil, and Boss Fix Oil. Set seven coins around the green candle. Make a path of seven coins from it to your candle. Set your candle on the farthest coin, facing the green candle.

If leaving your current job is part of your plan, represent it with a black votive candle burned without a holder (a "stubbie"). Dress it with Separation Oil. Your candle turns away from it, walking toward the big green candle.

Over the course of seven days, burn the candles in sections. Each day move your candle one coin nearer to the stationary green candle, pick up the coin it has passed over, and put that coin in the circle around the green candle.

When you are done, give all the coins to the poor. Do not keep them.

CROWN OF SUCCESS CANDLE SPELL FOR A PERFORMER

This spell for a stage performer requires a yellow offertory candle, a candle holder, Crown of Success Incense, and Crown of Success Oil.

Inscribe the word "SUCCESS" on the candle nine times in a continuous spiral, like a stripe on a barber pole. Dress the candle with Crown of Success Oil. Make up a cone of Crown of Success Incense. Before you go to the performance venue, light the candle, hold it aloft in your hand, facing East and say, "May all my works be crowned with success." Light the incense and say, "May all my works be crowned with success." Touch your finger to the oil, then anoint your forehead and the crown of your head with an upward sweep, saying, "May [insert specific details, e.g. 'my performance on stage tonight'] be crowned with success." Let the candle burn until one entire "SUCCESS" word is consumed, then pinch it out and go to the venue to perform.

Repeat each night until the candle is finished. If the performance runs for a long time, you may get more candles and continue the spell each night — or, after completing the work to your satisfaction, you may omit the candle but continue to dress the crown of your head with a touch of oil every night, always with the same prayer: "May all my works be crowned with success."

3-CANDLE SPELL FOR LOVE, ROMANCE, AND PASSION

You will need three bride-and-groom candles — one white, one pink, and one red — plus three bottles of love oil, such as Look Me Over, Kiss Me Now!, Fire of Love, Love Me, Follow Me Boy / Girl, or Lavender Love Drops. You can use one oil for each candle or mix them. You also need three squares of paper, a pencil, a black ink pen, and a red ink pen.

Before dawn on the first day, bathe in pure water to which you have added three drops of love oil. Pour the water over your head 9 times as you say, "Spirit of Love, i do this work for love and love only, that i may be loved by [name] as i myself love [him or her]. Amen." Rub upward only as you bathe and dry yourself in the air only. Collect a small basin of your used bath water, which has your essence in it. Dress in fresh clothes, carry the bath-water to a crossroads and throw it over your left shoulder toward the sunrise. Walk back home and don't look back.

At Sunrise, take the first paper and write on it your full name and your love's full name in pencil, without lifting the pencil from the paper, so that the two names form a circle and the end is joined to the beginning.

Inscribe the name of the person you love on the gender-appropriate side of the white candle, your name on the other side, and dress the candle with oil.

Name the two sides of the candle, saying, "Spirit of Love, i name this woman [or man] [your name] and this man [or woman] [name of lover]. As is done to this candle, may it be done to our thoughts." Place the name-paper under the candle, then dress the candle with your saliva, saying, "[Name of lover], love me as i love you. Desire me as i desire you. Come to me as i come to you. By my loving speech and tongue, be mine as i am yours."

Light both candle wicks and pray: "Spirit of Pure Love, i burn this candle in pure love's name that i may be loved by [name] as i myself love [him or her] and that [name] will burn for my love as i burn for [his or hers]. Let our thoughts be one. Amen." Let the candle burn 1/3 of the way, then pinch it out.

On the 2nd day, again burn the white candle at Sunrise, and say the "Pure Love" candle-lighting prayer. Burn it until it is about 2/3 gone.

On the 3rd day, again light it at Sunrise, say the "Pure Love" prayer, and let it burn out, even all the way to burning the paper with your names on it.

On the 4th day, start at Noon. Write both of your names on the 2nd paper as before, this time in black ink. Inscribe and dress the pink candle with oil as before.

Name the two sides, saying: "Spirit of Love, i name this woman [or man] [your name] and this man [or woman] [name of lover]. As is done to this candle, may it be done to our hearts." Place the candle against your bare body, at heart-level, saying, "[Name of lover], love me as i love you. Desire me as i desire you. Come to me as i come to you. By the link between my heart and yours, be mine as i am yours."

Light both wicks and pray: "Spirit of Romantic Love, i burn this candle in romantic love's name that i may be loved by [name] as i myself love [him or her] and that [name] will burn for my love as i burn for [his or hers]. Let our hearts be one. Amen." Let the candle burn 1/3 of the way, then pinch it out.

On the 5th day, again burn the pink candle at Noon, and say the "Romantic Love" prayer. Burn it until it is about 2/3 gone.

On the 6th day, again light it at Noon, say the "Romantic Love" prayer, and let it burn out, even all the way to burning the name-paper.

On the 7th day, start at Sunset. Write both of your names on the 3rd paper as before, this time in red ink. Inscribe and dress the candle with oil as before.

Name the two sides, saying: "Spirit of Love, i name this woman [or man] [your name] and this man [or woman] [name of lover]. As is done to this candle, may it be done to our bodies." Dress the candle with your sexual fluids, saying, "[Name of lover], love me as i love you. Desire me as i desire you. Come to me as i come to you. By the nectar of my body, be mine as i am yours."

Light both wicks and pray: "Spirit of Passionate Love, i burn this candle in passionate love's name that i may be loved by [name] as i myself love [him or her] and that [name] will burn for my love as i burn for [his or hers]. Let our bodies be one. Amen."

On the 8th day, again burn the red candle at Sunset, and say the "Passionate Love" prayer. Burn it until it is about 2/3 gone.

On the 9th day, again light it at Sunset, say the "Passionate Love" prayer, and let it burn out, even all the way to burning the name-paper.

As the red candle burns to the end, again bathe in pure water to which you have added 3 drops of love oil. Pour the water over your head 9 times saying, "Spirit of Love, i have done this work for love and love only, that i may be loved by [name] as i myself love [him or her]. My love is mine! Amen!" Set aside a basin of the bath-water. The next morning, sprinkle some of the bath water at your loved one's door step to mark it and then sprinkle as you walk to your door and mark it also. When you see the one you love, wear love oils. Wrap up any left-over candle wax in a red cloth and bury it in your back yard.

TYING A MAN'S (OR WOMAN'S) NATURE

Tying a partner's nature so that he or she is sexually faithful renders the victim sexually uninterested in others or, if interested, unable to complete the sex act due to erectile dysfunction, anorgasmia, etc. Typical spells of this sort are the nation sack and a knot spell called "taking his measure" or "tying his [or her] nature."

A regionally-famed candle spell from Texas that accomplishes this work is called "The Blue Penis Spell" and it utilizes a blue figural candle in the form of male genitalia. (A "Blue Vulva" spell using a candle shaped like female genitalia may easily be adapted from it.) If the couple breaks up and the spouse does not dispose of the spell, the person whose nature was hoodooed will thenceforward be unable to have a normal sex life with a new partner. Coercive love spells like these can be taken off, however.

Here is how a woman works these spells on a man:

Before going to bed with the man, the woman gets herself a length of ordinary soft white cotton string and hides it in the bedclothes. While the man is hard, she takes the measure of his penis with her finger, which measurement she transfers to the string. After they have sex, she smears some of his ejaculate on the string. (This can be done in the bed or in the bathroom.) Alternatively, she can get some ejaculate on a clean white handkerchief cloth. If possible, she should not have an orgasm during their love-making because she might lose herself in pleasure and get careless, and risk being "tied" herself. She also steals from the bed a few of the man's pubic hairs or underarm hairs, or, failing that, his head hairs.

When the man falls a asleep after sex, she takes the string and ties nine knots in it (some say seven knots). The knots are made starting from the center and working outward, alternating left and right sides until the ends are reached. Each knot must be activated as follows:

She forms the knot but does not pull it tight. When it is ready, she calls the man's name and at the moment he answers, be it with a word or a sound, she pulls the knot tight. She must then make an excuse to him, explaining why she called him. It is the difficulty of making these excuses, i believe, that has led many women to recommend making the nine (or seven) knots on separate occasions, tying one knot each time.

Once the string is fully knotted, some women wrap it up with the man's hairs in the semen-wetted cloth, making a packet.

With or without the cloth and hairs, the woman keeps the knot spell on her. She may put it in a nation sack and wear it under her skirt or pinned to her panties, anywhere beneath her waist. She may piece the knotted string out with a longer string and wear it around her waist. She may even thread it into a self-covered fabric belt and wear it thus amongst her clothing. When she is not wearing it, she must keep it in a locked box or trunk. The man must not see it or touch it. From then on he will be hoodooed and the only way for him to get this condition off is to undertake an Uncrossing Spell — or to steal back the knotted string and untie the knots himself.

A blue penis candle is a common adjunct to this knot spell. The candle is inscribed with the man's name and a command such as "Don't get hard with anyone but me!" It is then dressed with Stay With Me Oil, Follow Me Boy Oil, and Commanding Oil. The knotted string is coiled around its base while it is burned in seven segments over seven days. When the candle is done, the string goes in the nation sack, as described above.

Another way to work the Blue Penis Candle Spell is to collect semen on seven occasions and to burn one portion of the blue penis candle after each collection of semen and knot-tying, keeping the string coiled around the base of the candle when it is not required in the bed for more semen collection. In the end, there will be seven knots tied in the string and the candle will have burned in seven portions, although not necessarily on seven successive days. The string is then kept in a nation sack, as before.

HOODOOING A MAN'S (OR WOMAN'S) NATURE

Hoodooing an ex-partner's or enemy's nature fixes the victim so that he or she is sexually impotent or will never be loved again: It is a spell of revenge or hostility, in other words, a jinx, crossing, or goofering spell. Typical of this work is the Black Penis Spell to kill a man's nature.

The woman gets a black penis candle and warms it up, then presses her knotted string into the softened wax the same way it went on the man. She anoints the candle with Crossing Oil and sprinkles it with Goofer Dust. Then she lights both the wick and the string and lets them burn messily to the bottom, knotted cord and all.

The man's symptoms will appear similar to The Blue Penis Spell, but, interestingly, a sexual revenge spell is easier to take off, according to most root workers. The counter-spell is a Jinx-Killer or Uncrossing Spell.

GREEN DEVIL MONEY-BACK SPELL

Start on a Saturday. On a green Devil candle inscribe the borrower's name along with the words, *"GIVE ME MY MONEY!"* Write his name 9 times on a paper and cross it 9 times with the words *"GIVE ME MY MONEY!"* Place the paper beneath an overturned saucer, and put the candle, dressed with Pay Me Oil on top of that. As the candle burns, speak out loud your demand for your money in your own words and close with the phrase:

Green Devil, I SEEK WHAT IS RIGHTFULLY MINE!

Now take up the burning candle and saucer and retrieve the person's name paper from underneath. Hold the paper near the flame and say,

Green Devil, this is my command:
Until [Name] repays the debt he owes
  Compel him to feel the sting of his conscience
  Compel him to burn with the fire of remorse
  Compel him to taste in his mouth only ashes
  Compel him to dream of the evil he's done
  Compel him to remember his debt to me
      Whenever he thinks of money
      Whenever he hears the word "money"
      Whenever he sees money
      Whenever he touches money!
NOW, PAY ME THE MONEY YOU OWE ME, [Name],
or it will be hot for you!

Singe the paper a little, then put it back under the saucer and pinch the candle out. For seven days, light the candle, speak aloud the commands, and singe the paper. During this week you MUST also contact him somehow and ask for your money, firmly and confidently. If you will see him in person, wear Pay Me Oil on your clothes when you meet. If you write to him by mail, sprinkle Pay Me Sachet Powder on the letter, drag your fingernails down through the powder in wavy "snake lines" and then blow the powder off the paper. If you email, text, or speak by phone, wear Pay Me Oil as you communicate and state your command clearly and firmly.

If at any time during this period he makes a payment or repays the debt in full, thank the Green Devil for his aid and assistance, and consider the spell complete.

However, if despite your verbal contact with him and despite the magical warnings he has received with every singe of his name-paper, he still has not made any movement to repay you after 7 days, you can add to the words and action of the magical command. On the 8th day, which should again be a Saturday, light the candle and speak your demands aloud, as before. As the candle burns, speak out loud your demand for the return of your money in your own words and close with the phrase:

Green Devil, I SEEK WHAT IS RIGHTFULLY MINE!

Pick up the burning candle and saucer and retrieve the borrower's name paper from underneath one last time. Hold the paper near the flame and say,

Green Devil, this is my command:
Until [Name] repays the debt he owes
  Compel him to feel the sting of his conscience
  Compel him to burn with the fire of remorse
  Compel him to taste in his mouth only ashes
  Compel him to dream of the evil he's done
  Compel him to remember his debt to me
    Whenever he thinks of money
    Whenever he hears the word "money" .
    Whenever he sees money
    Whenever he touches money!
Green Devil, compel [Name] to run through the flames of Hell
    Until he falls to the ground at my feet
    With his arm outstretched
    And the money in his hand,
    Begging me to take it!

NOW, PAY ME THE MONEY YOU OWE ME,[Name],
PAY ME MY MONEY — or BURN!!!

And let his name-paper burn up.

BLESSING FOR A FAMILY ABOUT TO HAVE A NEW BABY

Get a pair of white Adam and Eve candles for you and your partner. Add a smaller white candle for each child already in the family. (Let's say there are two.) Name and bless each candle, carving the name of the person on each. Now fix the Eve candle with a "baby bump." Form a small ball of white wax and adhere it to the Eve candle's belly area by dripping on some more white wax to make her look pregnant. (Hint: the soft white wax from vigil candles works well for this.)

Dress all four candles with Blessing Oil and herbs sacred to motherhood and health, such as Motherwort, Angelica Root Powder, and Flax Seed, then draw a circle around the family of candles with Blessing Sachet Powder.

Speak aloud your prayer for a successful outcome to the pregnancy and light all four candles. Let them burn straight through.

A MOTHER'S GUIDING LIGHT FOR HER CHILDREN

If you have a young one in need of protection, you can use this spell to make your heartfelt protective spiritual work look like an everyday knick-knack display, hiding it in plain site.

Purchase a Guardian Angel statue in any style. Write the child's name and birth date on a small piece of paper or on a small photo and tape a hair of the child to it. Go to a crafts store and buy some green or brown crafter's felt and some fabric glue. Glue the prepared paper face-up to the statue and then glue the felt on. Pray Psalms 91 as you work. Trim the felt to the base of the Guardian Angel statue and no one will know what is under the felt.

Get an easel frame for a photo of the child and behind the photo, when you put it in the frame, insert two papers. On the first paper write out your prayer for the child's safety and happiness. On the second paper write out a copy of Psalms 91 in your own handwriting. You may add a pinch each of these three herbs: Angelica Root Powder, Motherwort, and Althæa Leaf.

Assemble the photo with the hidden papers in the frame. Place the Guardian Angel statue and the framed photo of the child on a book case, entertainment center shelf, or small table-top. Set a floral array and a simple white candle dressed with Protection Oil in front of the display. Burn the candle when the child may be away from home or in any kind of danger.

This work can be adapted for use with a family group photo, if you wish.

KEEP YOUR MATE AND BREAK UP AN OUTSIDE LOVE AFFAIR

Select figural candles of the proper gender and intimacy-level for each person, and of an appropriately symbolic candle colour for the work, such as red for love, pink for friendship, or black for the intruder. In this example, we will use a red Adam candle, a red Eve candle, a black Eve candle, and a love lamp to back up the work between sessions of burning the candles in sections.

The candles are inscribed and dressed with oils, front and back, Keep in mind that this double-purpose spell is to break up a love affair while returning a husband to his wife. Use Stay With Me Oil or Return To Me Oil on the wife and the front of the husband, and Break Up Oil on the intruder and the back of the husband. Sprinkle Love Herbs Mixture on the husband and wife and a mix of Red Pepper, Devil's Dung, and Vandal Root on the intruder.

Set the candles up as shown, and as they burn, walk the intruder away from the husband and walk him toward the wife. You may burn them in sections over the course of three or seven days, or stay up with them all night for a marathon job of work. If you burn in sections, keep a red kerosene love lamp, going the entire time as a helper light, to carry the work on while the candles are resting. Once the husband's candle is back where he belongs and the intruder's candle is a good distance away, place a sharp-edged tool, such as a knife or pair of scissors, between them to prevent their symbolic reunion.

A double-purpose Break Up and Stay With Me spell with a Love Lamp.

FIERY WALL OF PROTECTION SPELL

Here's what you will need:
7 purple and 1 black offertory candles
1 Black Cat Brand white cross candle
1 bottle Fiery Wall of Protection Oil
1 packet Fiery Wall of Protection Sachet
1 packet Fiery Wall of Protection Incense
1 packet Fiery Wall of Protection Crystals
1 Archangel (Saint) Michæl holy card
1 packet Graveyard Dirt
1 whole Angelica root
A clean white handkerchief
A small square of tin foil
A photo of the perpetrator. If no photo is available, write his or her full name 9 times on a piece of paper; if his or her name is unknown to you, write "The Evil One" 9 times on the paper.

Make the Fiery Wall of Protection Incense Powders into cones on an incense burner. Place the Graveyard Dirt in a china-ware saucer. Next, prepare the white cross candle for the Protectee. With a nail, inscribe the words "Archangel (or Saint) Michæl, Protect Me [or the name of whomever you are working for]." Dress the cross candle with Fiery Wall of Protection Oil. Dress the Angelica Root with the same oil and place it at the base of the candle. Around it, lay out a circle of Fiery Wall of Protection Sachet Powder. Now dress the 7 purple candles, the Guardians, with oil. Place them in a circle right on the circle of sachet powder that goes around the cross candle. Sprinkle them with a little of the powder, too. Place the Archangel (Saint) Michæl holy card among them.

Next, prepare the black Perpetrator's candle. With a nail, inscribe his full name (or the "The Evil One") on it on one side and the words "Keep Away" on the other side. Do not dress this candle. Place it off to one side, outside the circle of Guardian candles, on top of his photo or name-paper. Place the saucer of Graveyard Dirt next to his candle.

Light the candles in this order: The purple Guardians first, then the white Protectee within the circle, then the black Perpetrator's candle, far outside the circle.

Light the incense. While it burns, pray for protection, call upon Heaven for aid, and ask for the intercession of Archangel (Saint) Michæl, who guards Heaven with a sharp, cutting sword. Enjoin him to protect the one who needs protection with Seven Guardians, whether they be Guardian Angels or Human Guardians (including the police, if you think this will be necessary). Let the candles and incense burn until the black candle is half-burned. Then pick that candle up and hold it in your hand. Take the Perpetrator's photo or name-paper and lay it on the saucer of Graveyard Dirt. Set it on fire with the Perpetrator's own black candle and say, "Let your evil self be your own undoing!" When the paper has burned, turn the Perpetrator's candle upside down and extinguish it in the Graveyard Dirt, saying, "Let your evil works be your ending!" Allow the other candles to burn out.

Wrap the Angelica Root, some Sachet Powder, and the Archangel (Saint) Michæl card tightly in tin foil, making a small packet. Tie the packet up in the white handkerchief with four knots. Dress it with Fiery Wall of Protection Oil. To protect yourself, carry the packet. To protect your home, place it by your front door. To protect someone you love, give it to them to carry.

Carry the left-over materials and the saucer of Graveyard Dirt with the Perpetrator's ashes and his extinguished candle to a graveyard. Throw them against a grave stone, being sure to break the saucer as you throw this mess. Don't say a word; just turn and walk away home and don't look back. When you get home and everything is all put away and cleaned up, dissolve the Fiery Wall of Protection Crystals in water and wash down your home, while you recite the 37th Psalm ("Fret Not Thyself With Evil-doers ...") 37 times.

A SUGAR OR HONEY JAR TO SWEETEN PEOPLE TO YOU

Write the name of each person (family, lover, teacher, court official) on a separate piece of paper. Add a personal concern such as a hair, photo, or fingernail, plus herbs and roots appropriate to the situation. Fold the paper into a packet. Press the packet into a jar of sugar or honey with your finger, lick your finger, and say, "As [honey or sugar] is sweet to me, so will [name] be sweet to me." When all names are in the jar, seal it and set a dressed candle on it in a star holder. Burn the light each Monday, Wednesday, and Friday for slow but steady sweetening effects.

Read more sweetening spells (with and without candles) in this book: **"Hoodoo Honey and Sugar Spells" by Deacon Millett**

CANDLE DIVINATION TECHNIQUES

When we burn candles in the conjure tradition, we often watch and wait for divinatory signs that tell us how the work is going to come out — that is, whether the spell will be a success or not.

Some of the signs we observe have nothing to do with the candle itself. They may be dreams, natural occurrences, or so-called "coincidences" (especially names and ideas that relate to those in the spell).

We can also consult a formal system of divination, such as using a pendulum or a jack ball, reading or cutting playing cards or tarot cards, or employing bibliomancy (divination by means of a book such as the Bible).

Three other easy ways to get a divination on candle burning spells are through pyromancy (divination by flame), ceromancy (divination by wax), and capnomancy (divination by smoke). We generally combine pyromancy, capnomancy, and ceromancy into one art, which we call "reading signs from candles." Not every conjure worker reads candles, but for the most part, we do pay attention to the way a candle burns and can draw conclusions about it. In particular, spiritual workers who set lights for clients make a habit of noticing the manner in which the candles burn.

• Pyromancy: Signs Observed While the Candle Burns

Pyromancy, also called Fire Gazing or Fire Divination, is a method of foretelling the future in which the reader stares intently into burning flames or coals in order to catch a glimpse of things to come. Although it is loosely related to candle reading and candle glass reading, it is actually a form of scrying or visionary reading. You can perform pyromancy with a campfire or by watching the flames in your fireplace. If you watch candle flames for signs, you are also practicing a form of pyromancy.

An observant spiritual worker can learn many things from the way a client's candle burns. If the flame is hot and high, the work is proceeding quickly; if it burns low and almost goes out, there is not a lot of spiritual force behind the job, and if it gives off clouds of thick, black smoke, an enemy is opposing the work.

To perform a pyromantic divination with candles, it is best to work by candle light only, in an otherwise dark or dim room. If the behaviour does not stop, then it is to be considered a sign, and not simply a physical coincidence.

• Ceromancy: Signs Observed in Wax

The art of reading signs or making divinations from melted candle wax is called ceromancy or wax reading. There are two forms of ceromancy:

- You may dedicate a candle in a ritual manner, then pour drops of the melted wax from it into cold water, snow, or sand. The resultant hardened blobs of wax can be read just like reading tea leaves, with similar or identical meanings given to the images formed in the wax — a tree, a cat, a book, a car — that you will find in any good book on tea leaf reading.
- You may read candles used in a magical rite. In this case the wax is not poured off of the candles but rather the manner in which the wax melts, as well as the forms taken by the wax remnants left after candle goes out, are observed for signs. The melting candle wax creates various pictures and patterns of flow and design, which are interpreted to give information about the nature of the problem being addressed by the candle burning, the likelihood of success, and the obstacles being faced. The wax puddles which remain on the altar plate or in the candle stand are also interpreted by the shapes that they take as they pool, run, and harden.

• Capnomancy: Signs Observed in Smoke

The art of reading signs or making divinations from smoke is called capnomancy or smoke reading. There are two types of capnomancy:

- Active or "live" capnomancy is performed by scrying into the smoke of a wood fire or incense and observing moving images.
- Static capnomancy is performed by burning something — generally candles, matches, an oil lamp, wood, or incense — and passing an article such as a white plate or an inverted drinking glass or cup through the smoke, so that soot accumulates in or on the item. Alternatively, the fire may be lit inside a narrow container such as a glass lamp chimney or a candle glass. The smoke and soot marks left on the plate, cup, lamp chimney, or glass are then divined as images, somewhat in the manner of reading tea leaves, coffee grounds, or a Nordic egg divination.

• Cero-Capnomancy or Capno-Ceromancy: Candle Glass Reading

Candle glass reading is a specific type of divination in which a glass-encased jar candle, novena candle, or vigil light is burned for a desired outcome and the root doctor or home practitioner reads the combined traces of smoke, soot, and wax left in the glass jar after the candle goes out. Reading marks in smoke and soot is called capnomancy, and reading wax remains is called ceromancy, so the combined reading of smoke and wax could be called cero-capnomancy or capno-ceromancy — but most folks just call it "candle glass reading." The marks on the glass, made both by smoke or by wax, are interpreted as foretelling the course of the client's wishes coming true or spells coming to pass.

Wax and soot, along with other substances with which the candle may have been prepared, such as herbs, roots, minerals, or glitter, may be deposited on the inside of the glass jar and left behind as the candle burns down. Sometimes insects fly into a burning candle and are killed, leaving their bodies as markers within the glass. Additionally, on candles with paper labels, the label may char or burn, revealing a symbolic disruption in the picture or text, which is thus called to the root doctor's attention.

Often shapes, numbers, and other symbols can be seen both along the sides of the glass candles and collected in their bottoms. These images may form in the smoke or soot of the candle, or they may be comprised of herbs or glitter, in which case they can be read in a manner similar to the methods that tea leaf readers use to interpret herbs left in a tea cup.

In rare cases, the candle glass may crack or even explode. When it does, wax may pour onto the altar from the break, and it may also form patterns of spattering that can be interpreted by a gifted hoodoo psychic.

By reading these and other such signs, you or your rootworker may be able to perform a spell and a psychic divination at the same time.

In performing psychic readings on glass candle containers that have been burned on an altar, most rootworkers take note of when the light was started, how many days it burned, how much or little debris and soot remain on the glass holder, and how much wax was consumed before the candle burned out. These marks and patterns are analyzed by the worker, who is able to interpret from them various signs about the probability of the outcome of the work, and about the resistance or opposition being faced by the person for whom the candle is being burned.

HOW TO LEARN THE ART OF CANDLE READING

If you are a novice or home practitioner, you should not worry over-much about candle divination until you have burned a lot of candles and gained perspective on the matter. It is important for you to experience first-hand the fact that some candles are poorly made and will burn badly no matter what you do with them. Additionally, you will need to burn many candles in order to understand how the temperature in your rooms, the presence of wind or a draft, and other external factors may play a part in how the candles burn.

However, as a spiritual candle diviner, you can't just chalk up bad results to "physics." The fact that a "natural" draft put your candle out or "the cat tipped it over" or it was "badly made" does not obviate the fact that the candle going out was a bad sign. A sign is a message from Spirit and/or from the people for whom the candles were named, and the manner by which the sign was delivered is not as important as that you saw and received it.

By integrating both the physics of candle burning and the spiritual reality of omens, you should in time come to understand that the signs which appear during the burning of a candle do not reflect on your ability to do the work — that is, if your candle burns badly or goes out, you did not "botch up" the spell — but that, rather, you received a negative sign,

Self-taught practitioners who burn their own candles at home may not be experienced enough to interpret candle divination signs, but although professional candle workers provide interpretations of the way that candle spells turn out, new practitioners rarely take the logical step of hiring rootworkers in order to learn how to interpret candles. They tell me that they would rather try to learn from descriptive texts — but then they get confused and anxious when they fail to grasp the subject at once.

I understand wanting to study on your own, and this book will help you, but even if you don't hire a root doctor to set your lights, i do recommend that you schedule a paid consultation or two with a professional to learn the art of candle divination. Photograph a candle glass you have set at home or bring it along in person, then let your spiritual advisor discuss with you the wax remnants, smoke clouds, or soot patterns that remain.

Finally, i need to caution you that the signs made by flames, smoke, and wax are so varied that no book can list them all. It is your job as a practitioner to grasp the theory behind candle wax divination, not by memorizing long lists of supposed "rules," but by entering into a state of spiritual insight.

"SAVING BAD CANDLES" VERSUS "READING TEST CANDLES"

When a free-standing candle is in danger of drowning, i abandon my natural inclination to use the candle in an accessory rite of wax divination, and with an awl, screw-driver, or pen-knife i carve a runlet to save having to do the spell over again. Most folks will almost instinctively do this for free-standing candles, but there is hesitancy among new practitioners to save badly burning vigil lights. One reason may be that they lack proper tools for addressing a candle that is well down inside an 8-inch tall glass tube. This is remedied by getting and using dedicated candle tools.

Another reason newcomers are reluctant to salvage badly burning vigil lights is that they are just learning about smoke-pattern divination in the glass, and somehow they get the idea that signs in the glass are only valid if they develop naturally, without meddling. They think that touching the candle may mess up the divination. However, vigil candles are spell-works-in-progress as well as divinatory aids, and if the wick forms a knot, it always ends up smoking the glass — so why settle for a bad divination sign and set a second light when you can correct the candle as it burns?

I always remove polyp-like knots on the ends of wicks and remediate bad wick placement to forestall cracked glass. I use splint-wicks to relight candles that go out, making a hole with my awl as close to the drowned wick as possible, inserting the splint, lighting it with additional prayers, and watching it closely. If the original wick catches after a while, i use my hemostat to extract the splint-wick, in order to avoid a messy double-wick burn.

I trim, groom, and work my vigil candles to get the results i want. Many people don't — God bless them — but then they have to light more candles, until they get one to burn right. For me, it's like raising animals — if one falls sick, i don't just buy a second one to replace it. I nurse it back to health.

If you want to passively WATCH a candle burn, then let the knots stay, watch the twin flames, watch the wax run, watch the glass break and spill wax all over. In my church we call these candles "test candles" — that is, candles burned for the sole purpose of divination by wax or smoke reading.

If you want to WORK the situation through candle magic, you do not have to sit back and watch it go nuts with knots, runny wax, or out-of-control flames. Get the message the candle gives — and then rectify the unfortunate candle signs as you work. This is YOUR WORK, and you can make the outcome of the candle spell as good as possible.

SIGNS OBSERVED WHILE THE CANDLE IS BURNING

The following transient signs are only seen if you watch the candle burn.

• The candle flame flares, dips, bends, or gutters repeatedly

To be sure that any unusual behaviour of the candle flames is not caused by the mundane fact that you have set the candle in a draft, it is helpful to keep a few non-specific altar lights going in the room, so that you can truly judge the activities of the flames on your spell-lights against some simple blessing candles. If you have altar lights set, you can immediately tell if all of the lights in the room are "dancing" or if only the lights on your spell or prayer candles are affected. If the flames are jumping on all the candles, it may be necessary to close the doors or windows or to move the spell candles somewhere else.

- If a candle flame "dances" or "bounces" or forms a high spiral of flame, it is often seen as a sign that the person on whom you are working is greatly affected by the work; your message is getting through; watch out, though, because if the flame flares up too high, the candle may burn up overly fast or you may end up with a candle that flames up into a fire hazard.
- If a candle shows repeated flaring up and dying away or guttering of the flame, alternating between high and low flame, or even briefly winking out and then relighting itself, it is often seen as a sign that the person on whom you are working is subconsciously aware of your actions and may be responding partially, then fighting off your influence, then responding again.
- If you are burning two or more candles, named for specific people, and the flame of one tends to lean or bend toward the other, the person so represented is attracted to the person signified by the other candle. The one whose flame is taller is the dominant one.
- If the flame on a candle that was named for an individual leans or bends away from a named candle representing a lover or away from a central candle that represents some person he or she was supposed to protect, or if they gutter down, then the person so signified is emotionally repulsed by the lover or derelict in his protective duty toward the person signified by the other candle.

• The candle flame hisses, sizzles, pops, or makes other noises

A "noisy" candle is usually interpreted — especially by those in the Spiritual Church Movement — as a sign that spirits (of the dead, of angels, or of other entities) are trying to "come through," that is, to communicate. Pay attention! You may learn something important.

• A free-standing candle runs and melts a lot while burning

Some people try to influence the way melting wax runs. They do this as an intentional part of the spell-work, to increase the likelihood that things will go the way they want. Others prefer to let nature take its course and to watch running wax for signs, without interfering in its movements. Letting the wax run the way it naturally flows presents you with an opportunity to observe the flow of wax for signs. For instance:

- If you are burning a bride-and-groom type candle for love, and the woman's wax runs all over the man's, then the woman desires the man more than he desires her — and this holds true of all colours, including black for break-ups, white for new love, pink for friendship and romance, red for passionate love, and pale blue for peace and healing.
- If the bride side of a bride-and-groom candle — or a separate female candle — burns faster than the groom side — or a separate male candle — then she's more affected by the spell work than he is, and vice versa.
- If the woman's wax runs around the base of the man's, she's trying to cling to him, and vice versa.
- If you are burning a green money candle and the wax melts and runs down onto the monetary offering, then the spell is "eager to work" and the candle is "blessing the money."

• A free-standing candle smokes heavily but burns clean at the end

If a candle you are watching releases heavy bursts of black smoke, this is a token of hidden trouble or someone working against your wishes. As usually happens, these candles clean up toward the end of the burn and may finish just like a normal candle. This means that things will not go well at first, but with repeated work, you may overcome.

• A pin or needle on a marked candle drops, but clings and won't fall.

When the pin that marked a candle burned in sections clings to the candles, it means that either the client (the person for whom the candle is being burned, whether that is you or another person) is clinging to past conditions or someone or something from the client's past is unwilling to let the client go. The term "past conditions" means events, incidents, or memories from the client's past. The term "someone or something" means that it may be a living person (the client or another), or a hostile spirit sent against the client, or a spirit of the dead, or the spirit of a drug or illness.

- If the client is the one who is clinging, you will probably know it by knowing the client's case.
- If someone or something is clinging to the client, it is likely to be the same someone or something that is the cause of or is a part of whatever is the client's problem or situation that you are working to remedy.
- If you don't know which situation applies (i.e. whether the client is clinging to him/her/it or he/she/it is clinging to the client), you will do a simple divination on which situation is the operative one at this time.

Once you know which individual or situation the clinging pin represents, then you can address the issue through spiritual and magical remediation:

- If the client is the one clinging to the past, then cleanse the client by administering a Black Walnut bath to break ties with the past.
- If someone or something is clinging to the client, then give the client a cleansing Van Van bath followed by a Cut and Clear rite to break it off.
- If what is clinging to the client is very strong — for instance, if it is the spirit of a drug or a bad companion who hangs around — you may also have to do some Cast Off Evil and/or Hot Foot work.

Sometimes a pinned candle is intended to form part of a spell of cursing or attack — for instance, you may have stuck a penis candle with many pins to stop a man from seeking after prostitutes or online sex chat — or you may have stuck a skull candle full of pins to get someone's attention. These are not the same as marking a candle with pins, and in such cases, if the pins do not fall, the divination will be based on the puddled wax outcome, not the pins.

• The candle wick forms a "knot" or forms "twin flames"

When a free-standing candle burns with a "knot," "knob," lump, or polyp at the tip of the wick or breaks apart to form "twin flames" or two diverging wicks, you can get a good reading on the situation by letting it burn as-is, or you can trim the wick, which is what candle manufacturers recommend.

- On a free-standing candle, a knot or knob or lump indicates a stubborn situation with lots of intensity. The clumped-up knot signifies resistance.
- On a free-standing candle, twin flames — especially if they eventually rejoin — indicate that after delays a union or reunion may be foretold, or that there may be a flirtation, separation, or parting before the union or reunion of two parties.
- When a glass-encased candle burns with a knot, knob, or lump at the tip of the wick, the reading of the flame is greatly complicated by the fact that these formations will almost always result in a smoked-up glass, so that the capnomancy or smoke-reading portion of the divination can be expected to be dark, streaky, or sooty, which is not a good sign.
- When a vigil light burns with twin flames or two diverging wicks, either because the wick has split or because the candle was re-wicked and you forgot to remove the splint-wick when the original wick again caught fire, the smoke will almost always soot up or at least white-streak the candle glass, which is not a good sign. Don't let carelessness in the use of splint-wicks result in bad signs from sooty vigil candles.

One way to minimize knots and double flames is by trimming the wicks BEFORE lighting the candles. Some candles have very long wicks — maybe you have not had the experience of seeing these, but i have seen vigil lights and figural candles with up to 2" of free wick. Attempting to light a 2" long wick is just a waste of time — it cannot draw the wax up it. You have to trim it first.

Remember that a knot or twin flame formation may give different reading outcomes on a free-standing candle than on a glass-encased candle, due to the way we perform capnomancy of the candle glass in the latter type of candle. What looks interesting and ends well on a free-standing candle may look interesting but end badly in the glass of a vigil light.

• The candle goes out repeatedly or "won't stay lit"

This is a very troubling and frustrating situation. How you deal with it, and what divinatory signs you derive from it, will depend on the reason you were burning the candle in the first place.

- If your light was lit for simple increase or decrease without respect to the will of another being (that is, for more wealth, less illness, etc.) then this may be considered a bad sign — a negative reply from the world of Spirit to the question or aim implied in the work. In any case, if the light goes out, you will have to relight it. Do so with a prayer.
- If the candle was set in opposition to the will of another being (that is, as a coercive love spell, an antagonistic spell, etc.) then this sign may either be a negative reply from the world of Spirit to the question implied in the work or it may be a message from the other person, stating opposition, resistance, blockage, or reversal of your designs. Such a dousing of your lights may indicate that someone very strong is working against you or against the person on whose behalf you are setting the lights. In any case, if the light goes out, you will have to relight it. Do so with a prayer.
- If you catch the extinguished candle before the wax hardens, you may tip and roll the candle, allowing wax to run away from the wick and harden up higher on the sides of the wax or the glass.
- If the light goes out or is put out a second time, regardless of the reason you lit the candle, this a sign that you may need to use stronger means than you first employed to reach the goal. Try relighting it again, with a stronger and more focussed prayer.
- If the light goes out a third time, you should splint the wick. Drive a hole into the wax near the original wick, and insert the splint-wick. Pray over such a re-wicked candle very intently before relighting it. If the original wick finally takes fire, remove the splint-wick with your kitchen tongs or surgical hemostat in order to avoid a messy, double-wicked burn. Consider also that if you are burning a splinted candle, you may wish to add a second "helper" or "back-up" light on the altar.
- If no amount of effort on your part enables the candle to burn — for instance, if your splint-wick goes out and the helper light goes out three times as well, you should consider the need to start the entire job over from the beginning.

• The candle burns up overly fast

Generally a fast burn is good, but an overly-fast burn, especially when compared to other times you have used that same kind of candle or to other candles being burned at the same time in the same ritual, means that although the work will go well, it may not last long. You might have to repeat the job at a later date.

- If you have set lights for several people and one person's candle burns faster than the others, then that person is most affected by the work, but the influence may not last long enough to produce a permanent change. For instance, in a Fiery Wall of Protection Spell, with a ring of seven candles, that person cannot be relied upon to stay the course.
- If one candle out of a set burns out hours or days before the others, the choice of what to do is yours, essentially. Some folks would take it as a sign that the work is fast but not long, while others might take it as a sign but would not like what it signified and for that reason they would light another candle to replace it.

Should you light another candle in its place? Well, there are no "rules" governing this, and the best i can recommend is that you let Spirit guide you.

Which course of action you choose will be determined by your own personality and your level of activity or passivity toward the world generally; the level of your activity or passivity with respect to magic, omens, this ritual and its desired outcome; and other factors such as whether more candles are readily available in the time frame of the ongoing rite.

You might do a pendulum divination over the candle remains and ask the question. Or try a card reading. Or use Bibliomancy.

You might try handling it one way this time and another way the next time it happens, because, if you burn many candles, you will see such anomalies more than once. Eventually, from personal experience, you will understand more deeply how you wish to handle such events in the future.

What would *i* do? I can't say, because at different times i have handled this differently, according to the factors i listed above. But if i had any negative feelings about accepting the premature burn-out as a sign, i would perform a pendulum divination over the candle remains, with simple yes or no questions, to determine if i should set another light.

• The candle burns unusually slowly or "won't go out"

Sometimes a candle seems to take forever to burn, or there may be a little stubborn stick of wick at the end that keeps pulling in wax and just won't go out. I have seen some candles run 10 to 20 hours longer than manufacturer estimates, flickering at the end, but never quite extinguishing. This slow type of burn can necessitate dramatic watchfulness, but do not get impatient and blow such a light out prematurely. Watch and wait and observe what happens.

Generally a very slow burn signifies that the work is very slow in coming to fruition, but what that means in any given case will, of course, vary based on the purpose for which the candle was set.

- If you see an overly slow burn on a candle set for a positive-outcome petition, it means that some time will elapse before you see results, but if and when they do come, they will last.
- If the candle is being burned because you wish to end or resolve a negative situation, the candle's refusal to finish at a normal rate may mean that the target of your work, your opponent or enemy, is shielded or is resisting being finished with the situation, despite your efforts.

• The candle or lamp tips over and flames up into a fire hazard

If a candle or lamp falls over or flames up so high that it puts your curtains on fire or destroys a portion of your altar, you know you are in trouble. An out of control fire is both dangerous and a very bad sign in terms of spiritual workings. Once you get the flames under control and take stock of the damage, it is wise to accept that the event is a sign that not only will the spell probably fail, but there may be increased danger ahead for you or the person whom the candle represents.

- In order to accomplish any positive spell work, you will have to start the entire job over from the beginning — but before setting any more lights, do a thorough Uncrossing Spell for everyone involved and ritually clean the premises with Chinese Wash.
- If the spell was a curse, do a divination to determine if God moved against you, or if your enemy is stronger than you thought. If you were defeated but the cause is still justified, hire a spiritual worker to help.

SIGNS LEFT IN THE RESIDUE FROM A BURNED-OUT CANDLE

Transient images are those which occur while the candle is burning but disappear by the time the candle flame has gone out. Persistent images are those which are left in the form of solid wax after the flame has gone out.

• A free-standing candle burns down to a puddle of wax images

Wax puddles come in all kinds of shapes, and most candle-workers treat them like tea-leaves when they read them. Examine the shape of the wax for a form or token that may suggest an outcome regarding the matter at hand.

It is important, when learning this art, to understand how the meaning of a sign may vary, depending on the intention of the spell. For instance, a heart-shaped wax puddle is a good significator if you are burning a candle for a love spell — but a bad sign if you are trying to break a couple up. Likewise, a coffin-shaped wax puddle is a bad sign if you hope for health, but a good significator if you are burning a black candle against an enemy.

One transient image that often forms while a candle burns, but may disappear by the time it is finished, is a run of wax droplets down the side of the candle. These are called "tears" and they denote that someone will cry before the spell succeeds.

- If the tears melt away and are gone by the time the candle is finished, the sorrow will pass in due time.
- If the tears persist after the candle is finished and either hang down like icicles or form tall columns or spires of unburned wax tears, the sorrow will be of long effect.
- If the tears build up and arc outward to form persistent "wings," the person or situation is being guarded or sheltered by an angel, which is a very good sign — unless, of course. you were intending to cause harm.

• The candle gives a clean, even burn with no tokens or signs

This means things will go well with the spell or blessing and that one will most likely get what one wishes for. If a glass-encased vigil or novena candle burns and leaves no marks on the glass, that is best. If a free-standing candle leaves little or no residue, that is best.

SIGNS LEFT IN OR ON THE CANDLE HOLDER

Sometimes there are distinct images seen in the haze or soot left by smoke that clings to a candle glass. You may see an angel, a skull, a playful dog, a human face, a ghostly figure, or a heart. These signs, and many others, can be interpreted in the same way as tea leaf patterns.

• **A dirty, grey, black, or sooty burn marks the candle glass or holder**

- Marks on the front side of the candle indicate obvious problems; those on the back side indicate hidden problems.
- Grey smoke or black soot at the top which fades down to a clear bottom indicates that someone is working against your wishes. Things will not go well at first, but by repeated spells you may get them to go better.
- A scorched label points to problems in the area of the image that burned, such as the head, heart, or hand; or with whatever words got burned out.
- If the work is being done for love or money, grey or black marks mean that the subject of the spell — the beloved or the person who has been asked to provide the money — is "resisting" the work and "throwing up obstacles" against the person on whose behalf the light has been set.
- If the work is being done against an enemy and the enemy's candle burns sooty and dirty, then it is likely that the enemy is fighting your influences.
- Black soot all the way from top to bottom means things are going to go hard; the spell may not work, the blessing may fail, the person you are trying to help is in deeper stress or trouble than you thought.

• **Stuck herbs, wax, or glitter leave tokens or signs in the candle glass**

- Stuck items may form rings or patches. Rings around the glass symbolize delays and obstacles; patches are read as images, like tea leaves.
- Stuck glitter symbolizes shiny distractions or inappropriate attractions.
- A partial ring of herbs or glitter at the front means delays or distractions from known causes; at the back, from unknown causes or hidden foes.
- A ring of unburned wax at the bottom means unresolved past issues.
- Confetti pieces are read according to position and design; a heart or dollar sign stuck in a patch of herbs means love or money is blocked; a rising heart or dollar sign means new love or better finances on the way.

• The glass or ceramic candle holder or plate cracks or breaks

Breakage is never a "good" sign — but it is not always "bad," either. In a spell for increase or amelioration, a broken holder is unfortunate; in a spell of aggressive expulsion, the break can indicate the suddenness of the rupture.

- If the crack or breakage results in dripping wax, the indication is for tears or loss of blood.
- If the crack or shattered glass is "dry," the outcome is not likely to involve tears or blood.

Here are examples of how i interpret a broken holder as a "bad sign":

- On a Stay With Me candle to keep your husband from divorcing you a cracked glass or ceramic plate is a bad sign.
- On a Blessing candle to help someone recover from a traumatic brain injury in which there is a crack near the top (head) of the glass, i'd call it a bad sign — there will be a remaining deficit in cognition.
- On a Reconciliation or Return to Me candle to draw your ex-lover back, a broken glass or plate means he has split and wants to stay split.
- On a Love Me candle to cause someone to care for you, a broken glass and dripping wax means tears and separation and a broken relationship.
- On a Money Stay With Me candle to control your financial losses, a broken glass or plate with dripping wax means an inability to control outflow of your money, and thus the failure of your spell.

Sometimes the breakage is neutral, or functions as a warning:

- If you want to make a winning bid on a house that is for sale, and you set a House Blessing or Money House Blessing candle on a picture of the house and the glass cracks, i'd take the crack as a sign that there make be hidden flaws in the house itself. This is a warning sign to you — and as such it is neither a "good" nor "bad" sign — but heeding the warning might save you a bundle of money on down the road, which is good.
- If the candle is being burned in opposition to someone, like an enemy, for instance, the breakage of the glass or ceramic holder may signify resistance, fighting back, or a reversal of the spell.

Sometimes breaking a situation apart is exactly what you want to do:

- On a Separation candle to break your apartment lease prematurely so that you could move into a new apartment, i'd call it a fairly good sign.
- On a Separation or Break Up candle, a break might signify a very complete and abruptly shattered break-up (with tears of sorrow).
- On a Separation or Break Up candle, a break plus black soot or a burnt candle label signifies their break will be temporary or incomplete.
- On an Intranquility candle, a break may mean that the target is resisting or is shielded, or that the Intranquil Spirit doesn't wish to work for you.
- On an Essence of Bend-Over candle, a break means that the one whom you wish to bend to your will is fighting back and breaking your spell.

In some cases, the breakage is ambiguous and further divination is needed:

- On a Road Opener candle to break up a log-jam between your union and a corporation, there might indeed be a break-through, but not for the best, because as the wax ran out, so too might some employees "run out."
- On a Break Up candle to break your wife from her outside lover, a break may mean they'll split up, but not that your wife will stay faithful to you.
- On a Cast Off Evil candle a break might signify that the evil spell is broken — but if the evil is embodied in a bad person (as opposed to a bad habit or substance abuse) the foe may resist being "cast off."

The symbolism of broken holders varies based on the type of candle, and cannot be neatly summarized by a set of "rules." When divining, combine the break with signs from soot, wax, or a burned label, to get a full picture. Then, no matter what your objective, i would recommend that you set another of the same sort of light on the same situation; that is, i urge you to re-do the work because i would not consider a broken candle holder to be a positive outcome unless the candle was lit for a negative petition — and even then it would have negative side-effects, such as tears, blood, and loss.

Finally, the best way to avoid a broken candle plate, saucer, or holder is to not use glass or ceramic in this capacity. A worker who persists in the habit, especially after breaking more than one such article, is one who is ungrounded in the real world, whose spirituality may aim high but who fails to note the physical laws that govern and set limits on our Earthly lives.

HOW TO RITUALLY DISPOSE OF CANDLE SPELL REMAINS

Once you have conducted a divination on your candle spell or wax remains; recycled any candle glass; and saved unused oils, herbs, powders, or incense for future use; it is time to dispose of the remnants of your rite. If you did a one-time spell, you can dispose of unused supplies with the remnants. Traditional disposals are symbolically related to the intention of the work:

- If the intention of the spell is good and it involves matters around your own home, wrap the materials in a cloth or paper packet and bury them in the yard. Never bury remains from negative spells in your own yard.
- If the intention of the spell is not centered on matters close to home, or if you do not have a suitable yard, wrap the materials in a cloth or paper packet and throw them in running water over the left shoulder and walk away. Alternatively, take them to a crossroads — any place where two roads cross — and throw the packet into the center of the crossroads over the left shoulder and walk away. The crossroads can also be used for throwing out candle wax remains from a spell that does not personally involve you or if the spell is negative or influence-removing.
- If the intention of the spell is to get someone to leave town, divide the materials into nine packets and add Hot Foot Powder to each packet. Start at a crossroads near to where the person lives and throw out the first packet. Then travel in a direction away from the enemy's home, toward where you want them to go, and drop a packet at each crossroads you pass until all the packets are gone. In the country this might carry you several miles. In the city it would only be nine blocks, so city folks only count intersections with a light when they do this, or they count freeway interchanges to get some distance worked up between the packets.
- If the intention of the spell is seriously harmful, you can dispose of the material in a graveyard. The wax and other remnants are placed in a miniature coffin, buried, and marked by a miniature headstone with the enemy's name on it. When setting such a spell to rest, many workers also sprinkle a mixture of Sulphur Powder, Goofer Dust, and Salt around the grave, then walk home and don't look back.

For more information on ritual deployment and disposal, see
LuckyMojo.com/layingtricks.html

CANDLE SERVICE MANUAL
of MISSIONARY INDEPENDENT SPIRITUAL CHURCH

This is a brief course of training for deacons who conduct private vigil light services for clients at Missionary Independent Spiritual Church.

THE PRIVATE CANDLE MINISTRY

A private candle ministry is a particular kind of spiritual practice, in which a minister undertakes personal rituals or rites for the assistance of others, or to bring benefits to a location or place, or to offer praise or thanks to God or other beings in Spirit with the idea that through the minister's devotional and petitionary speech, reverence of intention, concentration of will, earnest prayer, and the use of a burning light as a focal point, the parishioners' desires and hopes can be conveyed to Spirit. The word "candle" implies that the work centers around a flame, and in fact some candle ministers also employ oil lamps, bonfires, or the smouldering tip of a stick, cone, or coil of incense.

Parishioners seek out private candle service ministries for several reasons:

- Lack of Dominion: Their family members, landlords, roommates, or friends may condemn candle burning or forbid it outright.
- Secrecy: They may be working on someone in the home or a friend who comes by; if prying eyes spotted a candle, difficulties would ensue.
- Efficacy: They may lack experience, spiritual focus, or perseverance to perform solo candle work in general, or this candle work in particular.
- Assistance: They may request a tandem or simultaneous setting of lights or have us set lights to back up spell work they are performing at home.
- Health: They may have asthma or other breathing conditions that mitigate against their having any smoke or flame in the home.
- Safety: They may have pets or children who cannot be trusted around an unattended open flame; they may travel away from home a lot.

When clients search the Missionary Independent Spiritual Church web site for information about our candle ministry services, they will find this page:
CandleMinistry.com
Please familiarize yourself with this material, as you may be asked questions about our procedures by folks who call on the telephone.

ALTARS AND ALTAR-WORK

Altars come in many types, from the ornate and adorned altars in magnificent cathedrals to humble home altars set out upon a small table or even a nightstand by the bed. Altar work is the term we use for any spiritual rite or ritual that we perform at an altar.

• Religious and Spiritual Altars

If a candle worker is a church deacon, reverend, apostle, minister, or bishop, the altar work that he or she performs on behalf of clients may be accompanied by the recitation of prayers, scripture, or Psalms. Every candle service ministry has at least one altar set aside as sacred or sanctified space where candles are lit or lights are set on behalf of clients. Many candle workers maintain multiple separate candle altars for different types of work.

• Ancestral and Family Altars

Spiritualists tend to invite ancestral spirits and the beloved dead to watch over, assist, and be present at the altar work that they perform on behalf of the living. They believe and teach that images or mementos of the dead are welcome on the altar because in their ministerial work they call upon the dead to look over, guide, and protect the living.

Workers in the various African Diasporic Religions, on the other hand, generally prefer to maintain separate altars for the living and the dead, and some adherents of these religions may go so far as to believe and teach that it is "wrong" to mix pictures of the dead with those of the living.

In our work, we follow Spiritualist church teachings and so we freely and gladly mingle ancestral images among those of their descendants.

• Working Candle Altars

Working altars are maintained for the needs and desires of a rootworker's or candle minister's clients. They may or may not be used for religious rites. Spiritual practitioners who set lights for clients on a working candle altar may ask their clients to describe their specific intentions and needs and to provide a petition paper or photo to be placed under the candle.

• Altars for Specified Conditions

Both candle ministers and professional rootworkers may find it useful to construct special altars for various specific purposes. The most commonly found of these specially dedicated altars are love altars, where the candle minister or root doctor recites prayers and performs magic spells for love, romance, and harmony; money altars where prayers of abundance and wealth are offered on behalf of clients; and altars for health and physical well-being, where prayers are said and candles may be lit on behalf of clients in need of uncrossing, jinx-breaking, protection, healing, and release from pain.

Not all rootworkers perform enemy work or cast crossing spells or curses on behalf of clients, but those who do may also set aside a space for use in dark spells. It is quite common for a Southern-style conjure doctor to place such work in the bathroom on top of the toilet tank or out in a woodshed.

PRAYER

Prayer is a manner of verbally addressing petitions and praise to God, to powerful spiritual beings, to helper-spirits, to saints, to nature-spirits, or to Spirit in general, however we conceive of such. Prayers are directed towards the Divine, and are deep expressions of reverence, intent, or supplication for specific purposes, generally on behalf of our clients.

Prayer work involves the speaking of prayers for the client's needs. The prayers may consist of recitals of set texts, such as portions of scripture. They may also be free-form in nature and be spoken extemporaneously.

The intent of a minister's prayers will vary based on the case at hand. Prayers may be supplicating, beseeching, imprecatory, wishful, affirmative, or expressive of the client's needs, and they will also reflect the minister's own preferred and accustomed style of performing spiritual and religious work.

• Prayerful Recital of Scriptures

Some spiritual doctors ask that their clients join them in recital of scriptures. Those who are well versed in scriptural prayer may prescribe supplicatory or intercessory passages of the Bible that they deem most beneficial to the client's case. This can be done in person or by telephone, either in unison or as call-and-response.

• Prayer With Recitation of the Psalms

Perhaps the most commonly recited portions of scripture are the Psalms of the Holy Bible. There is a long tradition of knowledge, going back to the ancient Jews, in which certain Psalms are prescribed for specific situations, either from memory or from a book.

Entire Psalms or portions of them may be spoken while performing other devotions, such as bathing, spiritually cleaning a home or business, placing candles on an altar, or suffumigating a room or person with incense.

We often pray the Psalms a specified number of times, for instance, reciting Psalms 23 twenty-three times while cleaning house, or Psalms 51 fifty-one times on fifty-one days for forgiveness from significant wrong-doing or crime. The Jewish custom of reciting specific Psalms over oils or water to fix or empower them is also found in hoodoo and conjure practice.

At the Association of Independent Readers and Rootworkers, you will find a complete list of the 150 Psalms with descriptions of their use in candle magic and other forms of conjure, with links to their full texts:

ReadersAndRootworkers.org/wiki/Category:The Book of Psalms

• Supplicatory Prayer

Prayers of supplication are also known as petitionary prayers; they are often simply called petitions. Whether recited by quotation from scripture or spoken extemporaneously and without rehearsal, these prayers ask a favour to be granted by God, by Spirit, by the Universe, by an ancestor, by an angel, or by a Heavenly agency. "Please help me" and "Please heal me" are probably the most often spoken supplicatory prayers. The Baptist Deacon's prayer, well known to all, is a form of supplicatory prayer.

An elaborate form of supplicatory prayer has developed in the Catholic tradition, in which specific saints are given "patronage" over various conditions and occupations. Novenas (a series of petitions lasting for nine days) are recited in honour of patron saints and special "saint candles," as well as oils, incense, and other religious supplies, are made for each saint.

At the Lucky W Amulet Archive, you will find an extensive list of well-known Patron Saints of the Catholic Church with descriptions of their specialities, as well as links to further texts:

LuckyMojo.com/patronsaints.html

• Intercessory Prayer

Intercessory prayer is a form of prayer in which a spiritual practitioner, deacon, minister, bishop, or a group of people with a strong calling for the work take time to pray on behalf of others, to intercede for them with God, and to mediate for them or present their cases before the Throne of Spirit. Each practitioner's approach is different, but those who take on this work as a regular service often set aside a particular time each day to beseech God on behalf of clients who seek help. The work is generally done at an altar, with or without the use of anointed candles, vigil lights, or prayer lamps.

Intercessory prayer may be performed to assist those who, for one reason or another, find it difficult to pray on their own behalf. It is especially sought after by clients whose loved ones may have gone astray or who may be in current and present danger due to illness, accident, military service, or difficulties with the law, or who stand in need of deliverance from the depredations of alcohol and drugs.

For example, if a client's son has been arrested and her spiritual advisor hopes that the boy will be able to make bail before going to trial, the worker may pray Psalms 71:4 on his behalf: "Deliver me, O my God, out of the hand of the wicked, out of the hand of the unrighteous and cruel man."

• Imprecatory prayer

Curses abound in the Bible, especially in the angry Psalms, which scholars call the "imprecatory Psalms." These sincere cries from the heart are very powerful prayers of vengeance, if spoken with conviction.

Psalms 37: The Psalmist prays that "the arms of the wicked shall be broken," "their sword shall enter into their own heart," and "the wicked shall perish [...] as the fat of lambs, [...] into smoke shall they consume away."

Psalms 55:15: "Let death take my enemies by surprise; let them go down alive to the grave."

Psalms 58:6: "O God, break the teeth in their mouths."

Psalms 59:12: "For the sin of their mouth and the words of their lips let them be taken in their pride: and for cursing and lying which they speak."

Psalms 109:8: "Let his days be few; and let another take his office."

Psalms 137:9: "How blessed will be the one who seizes your infants and dashes them against the rocks!"

• Extemporaneous Prayer

A prayer that is spoken or sung from the heart, without a prepared script or notes, is called an extemporaneous prayer. Although unrehearsed and improvisatory, it may combine concepts or wording borrowed from or inspired by scriptures, Psalms, published prayers, or gospel songs.

Extemporaneous prayer is generally delivered with dramatic presence and melodious "toning" in a rhythmic cadence and at a traditional tempo that is appropriate for the subject being prayed over or about. As a form, it can be used for many types of work, including blessing and healing, as well as cursing an enemy.

• Affirmative Prayer

Affirmative prayer is a form of prayer or metaphysical technique that is focused on positive outcomes rather than negative situations. For example, a person who is experiencing illness would envision being in a state of health and affirm this desired intention "as if it has already happened" rather than identifying the illness and then asking God for help to eliminate it.

Affirmative prayers can be improvised, recited from scripture, or adapted from the texts of religious traditions such as The New Thought Movement.

A favourite Spiritualist Church affirmation is to write a prayer on one side of a narrow slip of paper, and on the other side, Psalms 66:19: "Verily God hath heard me; he hath attended to the voice of my prayer." The petitioner then wraps the slip around the base of an offertory candle, Psalm side outward, glues the end down, and the minister burns the candle in a pan of clean sand.

Affirmative prayer may be used in conjunction with its opposite, the prayer of removal. The affirmative prayer is spoken during a waxing moon, at dawn, or at high tide ("As the sun rises, this day brings me abundant prosperity") and the prayer of removal is spoken during a waning moon, at sunset, or at ebb tide ("As the sun goes down, all poverty is removed from my life"). The logic behind this application is that God has ordained laws of natural inflow and outflow, and that by linking our prayers to a natural condition that prevails at the time, the prayer is given the added power of God's planned natural event.

When working long distance, some spiritual workers ask their clients to read or recite certain Psalms or affirmations daily, perhaps before bed, upon awakening, while lighting candles, or at some other set time.

• Prayer Chains and The Crystal Silence League

In church usage, a prayer chain is a loose confederation of people who agree to freely pray for one another.

A prayer chain may be a temporary aggregation assembled for a single purpose, such as to pray for an individual who is ill; a family that is suffering; or a city, town, or nation that has experienced a tragedy. The term is also applied to any group which meets regularly to pray for others, and at which requests for prayers are stated and prayers are made.

In modern times, many old-school physical prayer chain groups have made the transition to the internet.

The online prayer chain of Missionary Independent Spiritual Churches is called The Crystal Silence League:

CrystalSilenceLeague.org

HOW TO SET AN EMERGENCY PRAYER LIGHT

As a religious candle ministry, we do not turn away those in need. Anyone may telephone or email our church and request that we set a free 4" emergency light with prayers for present needs.

• A Name Paper, Petition, and Candle Dressing Are Required

- Write the name or petition paper and inscribe the candle with a needle.
- No 4" candle is to be set unless it is dressed with oil. No exceptions.

• Use Designated Star Holders and Wax Colours on Brass Plates

We have four candle altars in the church. There is one star holder per altar on a brass plate. Each plate has a paper label underneath listing designated wax colours for that altar. Please use only those colours. The paper goes under the plate. Keep the plates clean. If you do not, the built-up wax may run over and ruin our altars. Burn only one candle in one star holder per plate.

• No Candle Reports Are Sent for Free Lights

Free emergency light candle clients do not receive emailed candle reports.

THE PRIVATE VIGIL LIGHT SERVICE

These step-by-step instructions describe how deacons and candle servers conduct daily private vigil candle altar services for our clients.

• Invocation

Begin the day's candle services at 9:00 AM by ringing the gong outside the church with a brief invocatory prayer for the success of the work and for the needs of the clients on whose behalf you are working. Have your candle tools with you, including matches, clear tape, white sticky paper, pens, pencil, splint-wicks, hole-poker, tongs, small envelopes, etc.

• Exhale

In order to make room for new vigil candles, we must open up places on the altars. This is like exhaling before taking in a new breath.

- Remove finished candles from the altars and set them in boxes.
- Pull candles that need to be relit. On their white labels, write the date of the first relighting, with score-marks for every relighting thereafter.
- Relight candles, with prayers, and put them back on the altars.
- Fill in altar spaces with candles from outside altars, if there are any.
- Remove red-dotted sequential petitions and set them aside.
- Re-order the candles in the boxes by date and date-label the boxes.

• Write Candle Reports

For each finished vigil candle, we send the client a written report.

- Find and pull the candle's paper invoice from the wooden work basket.
- Open the database invoice section and find the invoice by number.
- Click the candle report button for that candle.
- Be careful to match invoice numbers of candles to candle reports, as clients may have same-named candles set on different invoices.
- Fill in all the fields on the candle report, including your name, the candle's appearance, and your interpretation.

• Reporting the Candle's Appearance

Use simple descriptive keywords and phrases, like (but not limited to):

• A clear, clean burn, like a pane of glass.
• White cloudy smoke or spirit marks (describe area and image formed).
• White smoky streaks, hazy all over; lightly smoky.
• Evenly light grey or dark grey and smoky.
• Grey or black soot at the top but clear at the bottom.
• A dark, sooty burn all the way down.
• Down one side (describe side relative to map or to candle front).
• Stuck wax and/or herbal residue (describe area and any pattern).
• Stuck glitter and/or metallic confetti (describe area and any pattern).
• Dead insect(s) stuck in the glass (describe species if identifiable).
• Unburned wax at the bottom (tell how deep in approximate inches).
• Scorched or burned label (describe area that is burned and how badly).
• Cracked glass (describe area).

• Reporting Your Interpretation

Be concise. Use keywords and simple conceptual phrases, like:

• Good outcome; looks good; successful; favourable; hopeful signs.
• Communication issues; hidden issues; unresolved past issues.
• Delays and obstacles; sorrow and tears; some problems remain.
• Candle went out and had to be relit; there is serious resistance.
• Possible enemy work being done in retaliation.
• Poor prognosis; you may need to do more work before having success.

• Sending the Candle Report

Candle reports are sent electronically unless the client specifically requests a postal mailed report. Each email is sent as soon as it is finished.

• Create the email report; double check to see all fields are filled out.
• Put the email into the Pending Email queue.
• Send all Pending Email.

• Transferring Petitions in a Series from Candle to Candle

Many clients order candle services in a series — generally 3, 7, or 13 candles, because we offer discounts on those numbers. As you write your candle reports, you will notice that some candles are marked on their white sticky labels with a red dot and a series number, such as "1/7" or "2/7" — referring to the candle's place in the series.

When you write a report for a candle in a series, paper-clip the petition to the invoice so that it can be transferred to the next candle in the series.

If you need a new photo, print it from the client's file in the database.

• Closing the Invoice

If all the candle reports on the invoice are complete, congratulations! Before you close the invoice, check that all of these fields are filled in:

- Order Puller (the person who lit the first candle).
- Date Lit for every candle.
- Email Date for every candle report.
- Order Shipper (the person closing the invoice).
- Shipping Method (Email / No Report Needed / USPS First Class).
- Ship Date (the date of the final email on the last candle).

• Mailing Candle Reports by Postal Mail If Requested

Please follow these steps if a client requests a postally mailed report.

- Print out the candle report page and the email message page.
- Fold in thirds with the address label out, tape it closed, and stamp it.
- If a "Discreet" report was requested, place the folded papers in a plain business envelope, stamp it, hand write the client's address, and write out our return address by hand with the sender name "Susie B."

• Filing Invoices

Unfold the closed invoice and place in the file cabinet by date. Paper invoice copies are held for three months, then shredded.

• Recycling Candle Glass

Place empty candle glasses in the recycling bin whole and unbroken.

• Inhale

Now that you have cleared spaces on the altar and dealt with finished lights, you can take a new breath and set today's candles on the altars. This work of "inhaling" is done in an orderly progression, as follows:

• The Order of Lighting Candles

Working in an orderly manner decreases mistakes.

- **Candles that have gone out prematurely are relit first.** Be sure that you have marked their labels with the date of relighting and score-marks for subsequent relightings. Roll the wax upward if it is still semi-liquid. Re-wick candles that are going out persistently: Drive a hole down beside the wick, drop in a length of splint-wick, pray briefly, light the splint (with a fireplace match or bamboo skewer if it is far down), and put the relit candle on the altar from whence it came.
- **Candles being burned in a series are lit second.** Be sure you actually have the next candle in the series. Place the transferred petition and photo (or a new photo) on the candle, and mark the invoice with the date lit. Check invoice numbers so you don't jump from one invoice to another if the client has two series of the same candle title.
- **Pending candles that have already been fixed are lit third.** These are dressed and cling-wrap covered candles waiting for lighting. They may be dated candles whose date has come up, tandem candles to be set simultaneously with client candles for which the client has called, and irregular series candles (for instance, set in A-B-C-A-B-C-A-B-C order rather than in A-A-A-B-B-B-C-C-C order). Visually scan the top labels of these candles. Pull their invoices, mark them with the date and your name, pray over and light them on appropriate altars, then file their invoices back in the wooden work basket.
- **New candle orders that you fix today are lit last.** The preparation of new candles is covered at length on the following pages.

• Preparing New Candle Orders

- Get the invoices for the day's set of new candles.
- Pull candles for each order, one order at a time. If you need to label candles, do so. Make sure you have pulled all of the candles for each order. Read the invoice over for any special or unusual instructions.
- Read and prepare the petitions. For regular clients, consulting the database helps you to better understand the work previously done or currently underway. If no petitions exist, make them. (See below.)
- Fold up, outside-label, and affix the petitions. (See below.)
- If photos were provided, locate them in the database, re-size them print them, and cut them to fit. Be creative! Collage photos together or integrate them into the candle label art. Use glue stick to affix photos.
- Dress and pray over each candle; bless series candles as a group.
- Side-label the candles with white sticky paper. (See below.)
- Candles not to be lit immediately are covered with plastic cling wrap and an additional sticky top label is affixed.

Preparing Petitions and Labelling Them

Clients are asked to send petitions with their orders, but if they fail to do so, you must write them. See the entries in "Hoodoo Herb and Root Magic" under Apple, Goofer Dust, Sampson Snake Root, and Sassafras; the two lessons on petitions in your "Hoodoo Rootwork Correspondence Course" book; and the Lucky Mojo Curio Co. love spell flyer in "The Black Folder."

Placing petition papers under a candle is traditional, but we need to be able to see the names, so we tape the papers to the side of the candle. Fold the petition and write the following label on the OUTSIDE:

- Surname of petitioner, plus the first initial if the surname is common.
- Label-title of the candle (don't draw a heart; write "Love Me"); this is necessary to avoid confusing and mingling two runs of differently titled candles from the same client during the same time-period.
- Name of the target person; this is needed because clients may set the same title of candle on several people, now or at a later date.
- A red dot, made with a Sharpie pen, is used to indicate any petition that will be transferred to another candle in a series.

• Every Candle Gets a White Sticky Side-Label

On white label paper at the top of the glass, between the labels, note:

- Invoice number and invoice date (top right corner).
- Red dot petition transfer notice, if candle is in a series (top left corner).
- Surname of petitioner (center).
- Name of target person — but note that this is only needed if the client is setting the same title of candle on several people at the same time.
- Series number (1/3, 2/3, 3/3, etc.) and/or date to burn. Solo candles are marked 1/1 so that no mistakes will be made (bottom right corner).
- Date candle was lit — and leave room for a relight date and score-marks if they become necessary (bottom left corner).

• Pending Candles Are Sealed and Get White Sticky Top-Labels

Dressed candles held in stock for a series burn are stored in boxes. They need plastic wrap to ensure freshness and an extra white sticky label paper on top of the cling wrap so that we can determine what they are from above:

- Invoice number.
- Series number (1/3, 2/3, 3/3, etc.) and/or date to burn.

• Check the Altars Throughout the day

Please attend to the altars when you come back from your morning break, when you return from lunch, when you come back from your afternoon break, and just before going home. Clean up wax spills, relight candles that have gone out, and remove high flaming splint-wicks.

Make it a point to keep an eye out for problems. You can help the other candle servers if you check invoices, storage shelves, altars, held stock, and your own work for anomalies, then report them and get them fixed.

• Trouble Shooting: You Have the Invoice But Not the Petition

Please rectify the problem and inform the order entry workers of the error so that they will not continue to make this mistake.

- **Trouble Shooting: Dates Too Old on Invoices in the Workbasket**

  - Invoice was not closed or filed — a minor problem; please rectify.
  - Candle went out on the altar and was not relit — please rectify.
  - Candle remains in held stock and was not lit — please rectify at once.
  - Candle was not made or prepared — a serious problem, please rectify.
  - Candle was lit, is gone, was not interpreted — please contact the client, apologize, and light another candle as a make-good at no charge.

- **Trouble Shooting: Dates Too Old on Candles Held in Stock**

  - Candle remained in held stock and was not lit — please rectify.
  - Candle is slated for simultaneous burn at a later date — no problem.
  - We held candles for a client who wanted a simultaneous burn, but the client never called and a month has passed — please call the client.

- **Trouble Shooting: Series Number Is Wrong; Series Is "Broken"**

If you find a series number that makes no sense — say, 2/3 in held stock and no 3/3 alongside it — the candles may have been burned out of order. Fix this minor problem by re-numbering the candle on the altar and the candle in held stock. Check the invoice to determine who lit the out-of-sequence candle. When you have a quiet moment, take them aside and gently explain the problem you found. Tell them you re-numbered the candles and everything is fine now, and ask them to try to always burn candles in numerical order.

To avoid "breaking" or "jumping" a series, always match candles in held stock to their invoice numbers, don't just look at the candle title. Some clients burn varied titles in one series, some clients burn the same title repeatedly in different invoices, and some clients burn several of the same title — but each candle of that title is directed toward a different target.

- **When Clients Call To Ask If Their Candles Have Been Lit**

  - Check the invoice workbasket, altar, and database for dates of lighting; if the candles are done but haven't been read yet, read them at once.
  - Check the day's work; the candles may not have been dressed yet.
  - Ask the order entry workers; the order may not be invoiced or paid yet.

HOW TO CONDUCT A CANDLE LIGHT SERVICE
by MIKHAIL STRABO

INTRODUCTION
By REV. ADELE CLEMENS
Pastor of the Divine Harmony Spiritual Church, New York City

Through the many years, during which I have conducted services in my own church and as a visitor in others, a great many people have asked if it were possible to get some book in which various religious services were outlined, so that they might use them in their own churches or groups.

This made me wonder why no such book had ever been prepared. For, from the many inquiries, there was a definite need for it.

Some months ago, while speaking with Mikhail Strabo, I mentioned this to him. He was quick to take the suggestion. He said, "There are hundreds of ministers and leaders who are in constant communication with me, I'm sure that they will welcome such a book."

This conversation was followed by others, until he decided that an all embracing book, that is, one that would contain an outline of all types of services, would be too large an undertaking.

As he had been present at several of my Candle Light Services, he suggested that a beginning be made in that field alone. He asked if I would be willing to help by checking the details of the services he intended to outline. Needless to say I was very willing to do this, and here is the results of our work.

I have never known of any one service that was more inspiring or enlightening, or more whole-heartedly satisfying to both the celebrant and the communicant than a Candle Light Service.

I realized that there was a definite need for some sort of standardized service for use by various churches, groups, and circles. Some basic treatment that could be used as a foundation for individual adaptation and treatment.

This book fills that need. It is not a large book as books go. But it is a complete and thorough one. It is as large as it should be, for it includes four basic services that can be adapted for use by leaders of almost any group. It gives the necessary information, tersely, concisely and understandably.

Any celebrant, after reading these four rituals, should be able to build on that which the book offers and develop something that will be individual, inspiring and deeply religious.

The history of Candle Light Services goes back far into antiquity. The first man that lit the first crude taper in the darkness of his cave, doubtless breathed a prayer of thankfulness to his own Gods, that the night had at last been transformed into day.

So we, who labor that others might profit from our endeavours, can thank God for the blessings that He has bestowed upon us, for the blessings that He is about to bestow upon us and for the blessings that will be ours in the life to come.

Now that we have the tools, we can use them, to His greater glory. Let us work together. There is much work to be done.

REV. ADELE CLEMENS
Pastor of the Divine Harmony Spiritual Church, New York City, 1943

IMPORTANT NOTICE

It is to be expressly understood that the purchaser of this monograph is to keep its contents strictly confidential. It must not be passed on to others, particularly curiosity seekers. In following this injunction you will help to maintain its value as a Service, and in this way you can continue to share in what should be a most inspiring and valuable source of spiritual elevation to the celebrant and the communicant alike.

MIKHAIL STRABO
Guidance House, April, 1943

PRELUDE TO THE CURRENT EDITION

This small orange booklet has been my inspiration for 50 years. I first acquired a copy in 1963, when it was 20 years old and i was a mere 16. It remained available through several waves of publishers, but fell out of print in 2003, and i believe i sold the last 100 copies through my shop. It is too good to forget, however, so here it is again at age 70, lightly edited, with love and respect, for the use of succeeding generations of Spiritual Church ministers.

REV. CATHERINE YRONWODE
Pastor of Missionary Independent Spiritual Church, Forestville, 2013

THE BASIC CANDLE LIGHT SERVICE

Since this monograph is prepared for the exclusive use of those who conduct services, there should be no need for any elaboration on the value of a service of this kind. Suffice it to say that a service built on the suggestions here outlined offers the celebrant an unusual opportunity of bringing to the congregation an experience that is dramatic, inspiring, impressive and above all purely spiritual.

If it is conducted in a dignified manner it will be something that all present will remember with gratitude, and each subsequent service will find a greater acceptance, a deeper appreciation and a larger audience.

The various services as here outlined are not meant for any one particular religion or any individual cult or faith. They can, with slight variations, be adapted to suit individual needs and the physical limitations of your meeting place. The Candle Light Service is something that will appeal to all people, no matter what the path they walk.

There is no arbitrary schedule that you must follow in planning your calendar. The service may be conducted once a week, once a month, or as often as you feel it will be welcomed by your congregation.

It is suggested that you permit as many members of your group as possible to participate. This always increases the interest in any service and develops a greater acceptance for the principles that are to be taught.

In a Candle Light Service, music is a most important adjunct, as it is in all services. You should therefore arrange for suitable music to be played at the various stages of the meeting.

Music should furnish the background for the opening, for the lighting of the candles, during the meditation and for the close of the service, as well as during the singing of Psalms or other choral effects.

If your meeting hall has an organ or piano, your problem is greatly simplified. You can then, by rehearsals, time the music to your movements and your actions. If there is no organ or piano, the next best thing to use is a phonograph or turntable attached to a radio loud speaker. It is best to have this phonograph or turntable operated from some place where the congregation will not see the records being changed or adjusted. The music can come from behind a screen or from another room, as indicated in the diagram.

Your next step is the preparation of your altar or platform. We give you a diagram that should be helpful.

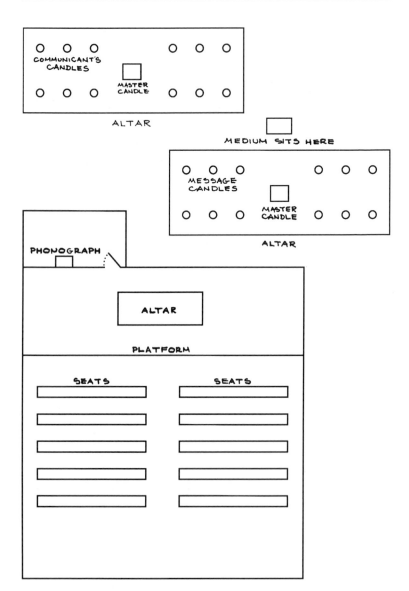

Spiritualist Church meeting hall, with altar layouts for a regular candle service and a mediumship message service. Art by Mikhail Strabo.

If your meeting room does not have a permanent pulpit in the front center of the platform, we suggest that you place a large oblong table there. If your meeting room has something that cannot or should not be moved, set your table to the right of this object. In the center of your table set your large candle or your Master candle, as we shall call it, in a suitable holder or on a large plate. Then arrange for several other holders or plates to be available for the use of the members of your group. It is the custom in some churches to use white plates of heavy restaurant-ware.

If possible get a large slab of some fireproof material, such as granite or marble, large enough to cover the entire table. This will eliminate the need for plates or holders, as the candles can then be placed directly on this fireproof material. As a further suggestion you might use a large shallow metal container which can be filled with bright, clean sand. Your candles can then be placed upright in the sand. However, as you read further, you may see reasons why you may prefer the use of plates for certain types of services, under certain conditions.

Around the large Master candle set a few smaller candles. We suggest that you do not put out all that you have, but rather keep a supply in reserve, and easily accessible, in a plain, unmarked metal or wooden box.

Some celebrants use various adjuncts on their tables or altars. Some use burning incense in a brazier, others use flowers in vases or baskets, others use one or two seven-branched candlesticks. You can, according to your requirements, use any or all of these things.

If you use a reading stand, put it to one side. You should not conduct your service from in front of the candles.

Now let us proceed to the actual service.

When you are prepared to open your service, and after the group has been seated, have the room darkened. It is preferable to have all the lights in the room extinguished. Then, as your congregation sits silently in the darkness, the music can begin.

It is best to use some simple music, simple enough to be played in the dark by your organist, or some selections that are readily obtainable at any store where phonograph records are sold.

As a suggestion as to the type of music that might be used with this service, we list the following selections. It is not necessary to use these compositions, we merely suggest them as the type of music that would well fit in with your needs:

César Franck — Choral No. 3 in A Minor
Alexander Russell — The Bells of St. Ann Beaupré
J. S. Bach — Passion of St. Matthew; the Brandenburg Concertos
The recordings of the Southernaires, the Ravizee Singers, the Soul Stirrers, and the Swan Silvertones.

You should have sufficient rehearsals in order to time your movements with the music. If you use records, it might be advisable to mark the sections of the record with coloured chalk to indicate where the music is to start and where it is to be stopped. We cannot stress this too much. Rehearse, rehearse and rehearse. There is nothing so distracting as a poorly conducted service.

Another timely suggestion. It you are using a new Master candle for your service, light it and let it burn for a few minutes before your service begins, then snuff it out. The reason for this is that it is more difficult to light a new candle than one that has been already been lit. The time taken in lighting the new candle might throw your meeting out of time.

After the music has been playing for a while, you are to make your entrance from the back of the room. Walk down the center aisle and carry a lighted taper. Walk slowly, in time with the music.

Hold the lighted taper so that your face is illuminated. If your room is sufficiently darkened, your entrance should be very dramatic and inspiring. You can wear whatever costume you wish. If you usually wear a robe it is advisable that you do so in this service.

When you reach the table, you are to light the large Master candle only. Then extinguish the taper and walk to your seat on the side of the platform, sit down and wait in silent meditation for the music to end.

It is most important that you rehearse and time the opening and your entrance. Arrange it so that the congregation will sit in silence for about three minutes, then allow about two minutes for your entrance and the lighting of the Master candle (of course, if your meeting room is a very large room, this section of the opening may take more than two minutes). Then allow about three minutes for your silent meditation. Do not have the music continue much longer than this after you have been seated.

As the strains of the music die down, rise and from where you stand, enter into the invocation. It is not necessary to give you the exact wording of the invocation. It is best that you use your own words. Do not speak from notes. However, you may follow this general pattern.

Ask that God's blessing be bestowed upon this service, that He look into the sincere hearts of His children who have assembled to do Him honour. Ask Him to read their intentions, their hopes, and their fears. Ask that this service be considered as a sacred request for His mercy, His grace, His guidance, and His help. (If there should be some special circumstance in your congregation or in your community, it would be fitting to include a special mention of this circumstance in your invocation.)

During your invocation, the only light in the room should be the light of the Master candle. It is best that you deliver your invocation without notes, so as to eliminate the use of an additional light which would take away from the impressiveness of the ceremony.

After the invocation you can ask that your congregation join in the singing of some familiar hymn, one that they will be able to sing without reference to hymnals or psalters, as there will not be sufficient light for them to read the words of a song from a book.

After the singing of the hymn, you can give the congregation a short talk on the reason for this special service. I will not give you a verbatim talk at this time, as you will not be able to speak from notes. I will merely give you a few suggestions on which you may base your talk.

Because this is a candle-light service, it differs in basic theme from others, such as the flower service, the healing service, the prayer service, and the thanksgiving service. Therefore you may speak of the mythical origins of light, about the light that comes from Heaven and now adorns this altar. There is a great mass of information on this subject in the book, "The Guiding Light to Power and Success" that you can use in your opening remarks. You can improvise, using your own words, and so come to the section where you will speak of the burning light in our souls, the reflection of the Master light which is the light of life. This book is replete with interesting ideas that you can use in your opening talk.

The motif behind this introduction should be descriptive to a great extent. You can develop the thought that many members of the congregation may have some special problem on their mind. Some problem to be solved, some particular burden on their hearts, or some anxiety over loved ones. It is this service's function to help them unburden themselves and lighten the load they are carrying.

You can then invite these people to come up to the altar or table and light a candle as an expression of their desire for their own particular purpose.

It is best to have one person designated to act as the leader of this section of your service. This person can come up to the altar and take one of the small candles, light it from the Master candle, and then place it on the table near the Master candle. As the celebrant, you may briefly pray with the petitioner as the candle is lit. The other members of the congregation then follow, one at a time, so there is no crowding at the table. They each light their candle from the Master candle and after placing it on the table they return to their seats.

One reason some celebrants prefer to have a designated person begin the movement to the altar is that he or she may place a coin in the plate on which the candle is placed as his offering in payment for the candle, and this will set the idea of offerings to be made. One preacher keeps a small basket in front of the Master candle where the congregation deposit offerings. However some preachers prefer not to suggest any offerings at this time. It is entirely up to you as to how you want to handle this section of your service.

You will now see the reason for not placing out as many candles as you had space for, but keeping a supply in reserve. It is not desirable to have unlighted candles around the Master candle. Therefore as you need more candles, you can have them brought up from your reserve and handed to those who wish to light a candle of their own.

After those who wish to light candles have done so, and they have returned to their seats, you can ask that all sit in silent meditation, concentrating on their desire and praying inwardly that their individual request may find favour in the sight of the Almighty and that they may receive the bountiful benefits of their devotions.

This silent meditation should continue for from three to five minutes during which the music can furnish a soft and appropriate background.

One preacher, at this point, rises and asks that the Lord may look with favour upon the silent meditations of the hearts of his children.

At the close of the music, you can rise and read some affirmations to the congregation. These can take the form of responsive readings. The leader can speak them and the congregation, in unison, can repeat them after him.

Do not make them too long. You must remember that your congregation will repeat them after you. They cannot read them from papers.

One preacher assigns the reading of affirmations to various members of the congregation, thus inviting them to become integral parts of the service.

Here, we give you a few typical affirmations. You can prepare any that you feel will suit the occasion:

1. I thank Thee, O God, for the bounty that Thou hast bestowed upon me.
2. God will point out the way for my earthly efforts.
3. I will speak health, I will live health, I will inspire health.
4. I thank Thee, O God, for filling my cup with your plenty.

You can add as many affirmations as you wish to this list, but a word of warning ... Do not carry them too long, as it may tire your congregation.

Following this responsive reading you can enter into another period of silent meditation during which period the music can again play an appropriate selection.

At the close of this silence, you can speak of the individual wishes and hopes of the members of the congregation, and then suggest that they take the remaining portion of the candle that they had lighted with them after the service has been concluded. They may burn the candle at home and in this manner continue the prayers that they had inaugurated at the service.

Bring home the thought that all these candles burning together can be a source of united power, a united prayer rising up to Our Lord and Maker.

Then comes the ceremony of extinguishing the candles. Those who wish to take their candles home with them should come up first and with a short prayer extinguish their candles and return to their seats, taking their candle with them. One preacher, rather than relying on offerings, suggests that they may buy their candle, the one they take home with them. It is snuffed, wrapped in a triangle of paper, and they are told that if they wish, it can be brought back to the next Candle Light Service and there lit once again.

After this, we come to the closing Benediction. Here you can once more ask God to look with favour upon the requests that the faithful have sent up to Him. You can then announce the date of the next Candle Light Service and ask those present to bring all their friends who would be interested with them on that occasion.

Then, in step with the strains of the music, you walk out as you entered. The Master candle should continue to burn while the congregation leaves.

Several ministers suggest that after the service, those who wish to, may be permitted to come to the altar or table where the Master candle is still burning, and there kneel and pray silently for the request that they have individually offered up.

The Master candle should be extinguished only after all the people have left the room. In selecting your Master candle, it is best to choose one that is sufficiently large to be used for several services.

MESSAGE-BEARING CANDLE SERVICE
FOR SPIRITUALIST CHURCHES

This service is especially suitable for Spiritualist Churches, particularly where the celebrant delivers messages to the communicants at the close of the meeting.

One preacher has found it most effective to have the Master candle in the center of the altar and two seven-branched candlesticks on each side of the Master candle. The communicants place their candles on a smaller table placed before the altar. However, it is not necessary for you to do this, you can follow the plan that best fits in with your physical limitations.

The service that we have outlined in the preceding pages may be used with some slight variations to meet your own particular needs.

The opening and the invocation can follow as they have already been outlined.

The first variation can occur when the communicants who wish to receive messages come up to the altar and light a candle. Each individual candle can be placed on a separate plate. In this plate the communicant can deposit both the question on a slip of paper and a token-object relating to the spirit with whom contact is sought. If you work with tokens, this method will do away with the necessity of calling for tokens in the midst of the service.

Some mediums suggest that the communicants also leave their free-will offering on the same plate. However, as we said, this as well as all other details are subject to modification according to your own plans and desires.

As the time for the delivery of the messages nears, the Medium or the Minister can sit in a chair behind the lighted candles, then, taking one plate at a time, can give the messages, according to how the Medium prefers to work. At the conclusion of each message, the Medium extinguishes the candle. The communicant should then come up to the table, take the candle which the Medium has extinguished, together with the token, and return to his or her seat as the Medium takes up the next candle on its plate.

One well known Medium suggests that the communicants take the stubs of their candles home, and there relight the candles for a number of subsequent days. Thus, in the privacy of their own homes, they can sit in silent meditation on their requests, in communion with spirits. This should be explained to your congregation if you wish them to follow this practice.

THE COLOUR CANDLE SERVICE
IN SPIRITUALIST CHURCHES

A number of celebrants prefer to use various coloured candles in their service. This affords the sensitive Medium the opportunity to observe the colour of the aura of each communicant and so suggest the colour candle they are to use. Alternatively, each communicant's needs — for love, health, financial security, tranquility, or clarity — may suggest an appropriate colour to the Medium, who will select the candle to be used during that meeting.

Working with a variety of candle colours also gives the Medium the opportunity of elaborating on the subject of colour and explaining it in all its spiritual meanings. It is most interesting to select a single colour for your dissertation at each meeting, and give your communicants some of the most interesting facts of Spiritual Colour Interpretation.

One very famous Medium, who conducts a well known church, has used the basic Spiritualist Church Service in the following interesting manner:

At each service, one colour is selected and the details of the evening are all developed in the light of this colour, its meaning, and its symbolism. The medium makes use of each colour's variations in hue and tint in the matter of drapery, vestments, altar cloths, vases, floral decoration, and of course the colours of the candles themselves. A Colour Candle Light Service should be colourful, never monochromatic. One way to demonstrate this is to set forth on the altar-table an array of beautiful, useful, venerational, and decorative objects in the colour-ranges to be discussed, and indicate them as you speak.

This type of Colour Candle Light Service can be organized as a series of weekly presentations. Begin with a general discourse on colour theory, embracing all the colours and their symbolism in brief, then proceed to each of the selected colours. Conclude the series with the full prismatic rainbow of colours convened, thus bringing the congregants to both a fuller appreciation of colour symbolism in a spiritual sense and to a compassionate understanding of the diverse mundane and spiritual needs and aspirations to be seen among their fellow congregants and humankind in general.

We give here a few of the highlights of the type of discourse spoken during a Colour Candle Service. As a minister, you can add to our outline and give as many details about the meanings of the colours and their spiritual implications as you may wish. This all depends upon the amount of time you can give to the presentation section of your Candle Light Service.

The discourse can be delivered in one session or over several weeks:
Now, as to the colours ...

Since all colours are the creative result of blending or mixing the three basic colours, which are Red, Blue and Yellow, let us consider these basic colours — but before we do so, we must learn to look at colours in the larger and all-embracing sense. Let us take, for example, Red.

Red is not a single colour, or a single density or intensity of hue, but a group of different shades of Red. It varies all the way from a light rose to a deep crimson. For your convenience let us place this group in a scale, something like this:

ROSE — RED — CRIMSON

Between the rose and the crimson there are scores of variations of what people usually call Red. Each of these variations indicates a degree of the qualities of the basic colour, more or less according to the intensity of the colour. The same is true of all other colours. They all exist in harmonious variation.

Let us begin with the three basic colours:

RED, our first colour, is called the colour of the life force.

Red represents all our life processes and activities, from the purest motives to the basest. The rose shade is the highest manifestation of this colour. It is the apex of the red group. It represents altruistic love of mankind, charitable love, healing love, forgiving love, the love of perfected humankind for the creator. As the colour moves along to the pure red, it indicates pure health, vitality, virility, and physical vigour. Further along, the shade grows darker, from cherry-red to scarlet, garnet, and crimson, which indicates bestial passion, and the baser forms of the bright manifestations.

Red is the colour group of love, passion, and ardor in its various stages, from the pure selfless love of rose to the uncontrollable anger, violence, and lust of blood-red. Red indicates life force. It also indicates strength and mastery. Red is love and God is love. It is the Blood of Christ; see Revelations 7, 13:4. It is the attainment of life's ambitions, the struggling with the forces that are around us before we can master these forces. Red is the colour of passionate sexuality, but people who become angry also "see red." This is an indication that we must struggle to overcome our negative passions before we can achieve masterful love. Red is the colour of Mars and of iron rust. It is also used as the indication of spiritual progress. Red is used in Spiritual healing to overcome anemia or diseases of the blood.

BLUE is our second basic colour. It is the colour of spirituality.

Blue ranges from the light faint shades of sea spray and periwinkle with tinges of lavender-purple to the brightness of cyan, and thence to rich cobalt, deep indigo, somber navy, and darkest midnight blue. It extends from the pomposity of purplish-blue, with its admiration and love of form, of show or ceremony, up through the foundational religiosity of lapis, and the sacredness of shamanic turquoise, to the clear cerulean sky blue of pure spirituality, and down again to the deep dark blue of depression and superstitious fear.

Blue is the colour of devotion. It is the colour of supreme faith. It is the colour of mental poise. It is the symbol of the waters of life, the beginning. Blue is an indication of one's arrival at a higher plane in this life. Witness the phrase "blue blood," which is used to indicate nobility or royalty. In spiritual thought, medium blue is used to indicate that nobility or royalty of the individual who through struggle, study, and meditation has at long last reached a higher plane of understanding and attainment, while sky blue is a significator of spiritual healing and peace.

YELLOW, our third basic colour, indicates intellectual effort and mastery.

Yellow runs the scale from pale straw yellow through sunshine yellow and gold to the ranges of yellow-orange that border upon red-orange; from active mentality and universal generosity to the selfish animal instincts. Yellow is the colour of intellectual power and successful mental activity. It is the colour of the Sun at noon, and as the Sun universally warms our earthly lives, so have many people worshipped the Sun and expressed this love in lives of devotion, loyalty, and generosity.

Yellow is the colour of the halos of the angels and saints. It indicates their spiritual power and activity, and their praise of their Creator. Yellow is the colour of gold, and just as gold, which does not tarnish, is presumed to be the highest form of metal, so yellow is a colour that represents the highest form of spiritual power, success, and attainment. Yellow is the colour of the flame of the candle by which we meditate and in which we see the fulfillment of our desires. In Spiritual healing services, yellow is the colour that is used to cure headaches.

Now having covered the three basic colours, also known as the primary colours, we come to the first combination colours. These are known as the secondary colours. In these combinations we not only combine the colours, but also their spiritual attributes.

GREEN, our first secondary colour, is gotten by mixing yellow and blue.

Green in its scale as a colour runs from the light green of Spring verdure, indicative of sympathy, understanding, and charity, through the bright green that indicates love of the outdoors, nature, and the wild, to the dark greens, forest greens, and hunter greens that indicate diplomacy, tact, and economic stability, to the murky greens and the acidic greens that are the sign of insincerity, falsehood, trickery, malice, jealousy, and deceit.

Green is the colour of development. It blends the intellectual force of yellow with the spiritual force of blue. It is the colour of growth on all planes. It represents the spirit of all growing things. It is a feminine colour, and represents the middle note of nature. The growing, the fulfillment, the leaf and fruit of the crop, the sign of life, the fruit of wisdom. It is the colour that indicates worldly power and property. It represents the reward for our season of toil, struggle, and application. It is the colour of our earthly and spiritual reward. In Spiritual healing, green indicates generation and regeneration on the material plane, especially in matters of financial abundance.

ORANGE, our next colour, is obtained by combining yellow and red.

Orange is the colour that we usually associate with physical vitality, youth, communication, and health. Looking at our colour chart, we see it run from the lightest tinges of warm yellow-gold and golden orange to the deepest and darkest variants of pumpkin orange, burnt-orange, and orange-red. This is an indication of the state of one's physical health, from the fragile through to the virile, to the baser manifestations of this group.

Orange combines the powers and the qualities of the yellow and red group, each in a lesser degree. That is, it is the colour that combines intellectual vitality and love, resulting in communicative speech, which, although a lesser force than that of physical exertion, can subtly change events in mighty ways. Asian teachers say that golden-yellow Prana, which we take into ourselves as we sleep, transmutes within the body to red, and thus colours our blood, and orange represents that pranic transmutation. It is the colour of the rising and setting Sun which brings to us the life force through changing days. Orange is one of the best colours on which to meditate for pure spiritual attainment.

PURPLE, our next colour, is formed by combining red and blue.

Purple or, as some people call this colour, Violet, is the colour of healing and helping others, by means of the forces within us. It is the colour of the power that we draw from the higher planes. This colour, too, has its range of shades, and its powers wax and wane with the intensity of the shade.

Purple is the royal colour. It is the colour that is highly esteemed by spiritual healers for its inherent power and strengthening qualities. This is the colour that attracts all that is good and beneficent from the higher spiritual planes. It is the colour of deep spiritual understanding, the colour that signifies royalty or aristocracy of the mind and thus rulership, authority, and control in this world. It is the colour that penetrates to the very core of things. Witness the violet rays, with their healing and penetrating qualities.

These six basic colours, the primary and secondary classifications, give us our basic interpretations. These basic colours give us the foundation on which to build our conception and understanding of all the other shades in the spectrum.

From this point on we can go into the thousand and one variations of the tints, from the pastels formed by the addition of white to the darker shades formed by the inclusion of black. A little analysis on your own part will help you develop all the characteristics of the tints. As a beginning, let us outline two additional tints that may act as a guide for you.

BROWN is a vital colour. It is compared with the earth which is the material source of the things that sustain us in our physical manifestation. It is the colour of humility, of the effacement of self in the desire to reach higher attainment. It is a transformation into a new life. Witness the leaves that turn brown in the fall, a preparation for their long sleep, so that they may emerge once again, fresh, revitalized, and new in spirit.

Brown is symbolic of the magnetism that we exude, that attracts us to others, that attracts others to us, the magnetism that is so necessary to us all. It is, above all, the creative colour of reality.

PINK is the colour of emotional success. It is red blended with white. It is the colour of friendship, the sign of conquering one's baser passions through the admixture of spirituality. It is romantic and reconciliatory. It is a new, fresh, live, and warm colour, one that means purity of intentions and honesty in one's aim. It is the colour of truth. Success is truth, just as failure is error.

We hear of people looking at life through rose coloured glasses. It is the pink in the rose colour that gives life its delicate, delightful, and fascinating aspect. It represents the vision of truth, the vision of emotional success, the love that warms and cheers the heart.

This brings us to the two important shades, black and white. Note, we did not call them colours. Black is the absence of all colour, while white might be termed the spiritual blending of all colours.

BLACK is the colour of mourning and weeping.

Black indicates our initiation into a higher plane. It represents a change from one state to another. Symbolically and in reality, it absorbs all other colours. The black candle that we burn for a spirit who has passed on is the flame that burns the tie that holds the departed spirit to the earth. It is the all effacing colour, as it absorbs and effaces all colours. It is the end of one plane and the beginning of another. The Alpha and Omega. The beginning and the end. It contains all and everything. Black in its symbolic sense can also indicate negativity in thought, deed, and emotion. It can represent fear, depressive ideas, and lack of courage. It is the negative pole of all thought.

As a suggestion, it might be a very proper gesture to burn one black candle at all your services. This candle will resonate with the sorrows of those in darkness, It may also remind the communicants of their departed ones and will be the flame that releases them from their earthly chains.

WHITE is the positive pole of all thought.

White is the shade that reflects all colours. It represents purity and faith in all things. For a special request, white may be used with any other colour of candle colour, for its added strength and power. By its reflection of the companion colour, additional power is added to the request or prayer.

Angels are pictured as clothed in white. Spirit manifestations are white. This is evidenced because white is the shade that indicates the vibration of Spirit. White is also an indication of the purity of our intentions. That is another reason it is often used in association with a candle of a particular colour. White is the shade of the highest plane. It is usually taken to be the sign of a master. Pure white is a shade that is rarely, if ever, found in this life. What we call white is usually tinged with another colour, such as yellow, blue, or violet. One white candle at every service symbolizes the world of Spirit.

THE RAINBOW or prism represents all colours and to this complete range of colours, we may add white at one end, and at the opposite end we may add black. And as we understand that the end is but the beginning, just as the beginning is always the end, we will find these two shades alongside one another, the blending of solid black into the purest white.

After this short explanation of the spiritual philosophy of colours, during which the celebrant can elaborate on any or all of the colours, we come to the close of this section of the service. From this point the ceremony can follow our pattern or you can introduce a variation of the ceremony that has been previously outlined.

A CANDLE LIGHT SERVICE
TO EMBRACE GOODWILL AND FORGIVENESS

The following ceremony can be a most interesting variation of the formal Candle Light Service. In this variation the participants unite in forgiving their enemies and radiate good will to all the world.

This Service was suggested to me by a most remarkable Practitioner who is well known on both sides of our country for the wonderful works she has instituted. She conducted this service in her home on New Year's Eve, some years ago, and I pass it on to you, in the hope that you may find this particular service suitable to your needs.

The altar is provided with three large candles and several metal containers filled with sand, placed in front of the candles. Three small pieces of paper and one pew-pencil are needed for each congregant. A box of offertory candles is at hand, along with clear tape.

At the opening, the celebrant lights the three large candles on the altar. These are the candles of the Trinity — the Father, the Son and the Holy Ghost. In a non-denominational service, these candles could be interpreted as symbolic of the Master, the Servant and the Spirit, or of the Past, the Present, and the Future. A short prayer is said over each candle.

The lighting of the candles is followed by a discourse by the celebrant on the Law of Forgiveness. It is not necessary for me to give you any details on this subject. The true spirit knows full well the importance of this law and its relation to humans. You must stress the importance of this message in order that the spirit of the service should be of some help to each of the participants.

After the discourse, two small pieces of paper and one pew-pencil are supplied to each of the participants.

They are asked to write on the first paper the laws of God that each has transgressed. In this way they are to ask for forgiveness for their transgressions. The motto for this section of the service should be the message of "First cast the mote from thine own eye."

Then, on the second sheet of paper, the communicants are asked to set down all the items of malice that were being held in their hearts against any one. There is no time limitation on the items of malice. They can come from as far back as they can remember. They are also requested to write down the names of their so-called enemies, and then call on the Law of Forgiveness for all collectively.

These papers are then all placed in a metal bowl, where they are burned.

The celebrant explains, "If thou bringest thy gift to the altar and rememberest that thy brother has naught against thee, leave there thy gift (your wish) and go and make peace with thy brother." During the burning of the papers, inspirational music is played. This is followed by a brief period of silent meditation as the transgressions and items of malice are released.

The communicants are next instructed to write their wishes on the third piece of paper, during which time there is more music, and the celebrant sits silently radiating spiritual help to each of the communicants.

An altar light is then given to each person present. A strip of Scotch tape is placed around the center of the candle. By means of this tape the participants attach their wish to their candle.

Then, as the music furnishes a background of harmony, the communicants come up to the altar, light their candles from the Master candles and place them upright in the sand.

(A variation of this part of the ritual, could be with the celebrant holding one of the Master candles. This candle represents the "Christ light." As each person comes to the altar, they light their own "Christ light" from the celebrant's candle, lighting it to the Glory of God.)

A silent blessing is pronounced on each of the communicants as they light their candles. They then return to their own seats. There is another period of silence, during which there is some more music.

Then follows the benediction, and the service is brought to a close.

The candles are left to burn themselves down, sending the written wishes up with their flame.

POSTLUDE

The compiler of this monograph would like to hear from those readers who will apply any of these services to their own particular needs. If there is something that you use as an individual touch to the service, or if you find in your experience some variations on the colour indications as we have outlined them, please let us know. We are anxious to keep our records on this phase of spirituality complete. It is only the experience of our friends that will enable us to keep it so.

MIKHAIL STRABO